OBJECTIVE
first certificate
Second Edition

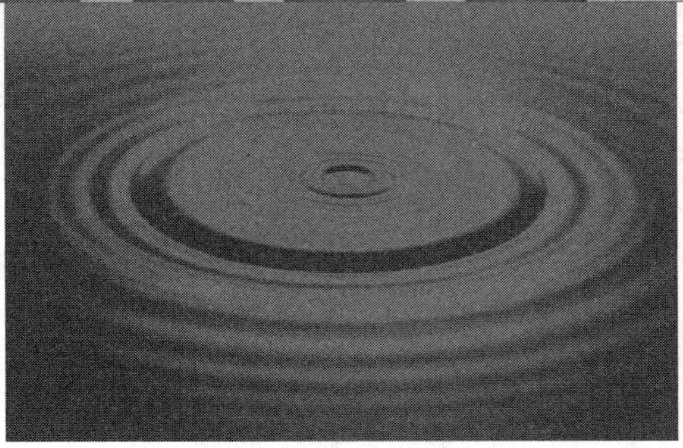

Annette Capel Wendy Sharp **Workbook with Answers**

CAMBRIDGE UNIVERSITY PRESS
Cambridge, New York, Melbourne, Madrid, Cape Town, Singapore, São Paulo, Delhi

Cambridge University Press
The Edinburgh Building, Cambridge CB2 8RU, UK

www.cambridge.org
Information on this title: www.cambridge.org/9780521700672

© Cambridge University Press, 2008

This publication is in copyright. Subject to statutory exception
and to the provisions of relevant collective licensing agreements,
no reproduction of any part may take place without the written
permission of Cambridge University Press.

First published 2000
12th printing 2006
Second edition published 2008

Printed in Italy by Legoprint S.p.A.

A catalogue for this book is available from the British Library

Library of Congress Cataloguing in Publication data

ISBN 978-0-521-70067-2 Workbook with Answers
ISBN 978-0-521-70066-5 Workbook
ISBN 978-0-521-70063-4 Student's Book
ISBN 978-0-521-70064-1 Self-study Student's Book
ISBN 978-0-521-70065-8 Teacher's Book
ISBN 978-0-521-70069-6 Audio CD set

Cover concept by Dale Tomlinson and design by Jo Barker

Produced by Kamae Design, Oxford

Contents

Unit 1 Fashion matters	4
Unit 2 The virtual world	6
Unit 3 Going places	8
Unit 4 Our four-legged friends	10
Unit 5 Fear and loathing	12
Unit 6 What if?	14
Unit 7 Life's too short	16
Unit 8 Downshifting	18
Unit 9 The hard sell	20
Unit 10 The final frontier	22
Unit 11 Like mother, like daughter	24
Unit 12 A great idea	26
Unit 13 Education for life	28
Unit 14 Career moves	30
Unit 15 Too many people?	32
Unit 16 Eat to live	34
Unit 17 Collectors and creators	36
Unit 18 What's in a book?	38
Unit 19 An apple a day …	40
Unit 20 No place to hide	42
Unit 21 To have and have not	44
Unit 22 A little night music	46
Unit 23 Unexpected events	48
Unit 24 Priceless or worthless?	50
Unit 25 Urban decay, suburban hell	52
Unit 26 Getting around	54
Unit 27 Material girl	56
Unit 28 Sense and sensitivity	58
Unit 29 Newshounds	60
Unit 30 Anything for a laugh	62
Answer key	65

1 Fashion matters

Vocabulary
Spellcheck

1 *Clothes Show Live* is a huge fashion exhibition that takes place every December in Birmingham. Read this extract from the catalogue proofs. Check the spelling before it goes to print! An example is given. There are ten more errors to correct.

STANDS IN HALL 6

 For a career in ~~modeling~~ *modelling*. You could become the next supermodel!

 Get some free advice on your hairstile. Make-up demonstrations too.

 The brightest and most outragous designer bags! Fantastic headgear too, including berets, caps and hats.

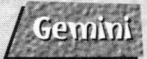 Gemini makes beautiful jewelery from crystals and gemstones, including braclets, earings and pendants. And it's less expensiv than you might think!

 An exiting range of leather clothing, from casual jackets to the smartest suites. Watches, belts, bags and sunglasses also available.

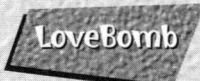 Unisex clubwear for the really fashion-conscius, with diferent abstract prints that glow in the dark!

Corpus spot

Think carefully when to use double consonants – the *Cambridge Learner Corpus* shows FCE candidates often make mistakes with these.

It was **impossible** to find a pair in my size.
NOT It was ~~imposible~~ to find a pair in my size.

2 Correct the spelling errors in these sentences written by FCE candidates.

a You can immagine how excited I was.
b There is a beautifull view from up there.
c The concert was briliant.
d This was only the beggining.
e Acording to the writer, it is expensive.
f They did not apologise for this.
g I hope you weren't dissapointed?
h Hapiness is the most important thing.

Phrasal verbs

3 Complete these sentences using a suitable phrasal verb in an appropriate form. Choose from the list below, which includes some more phrasal verbs to do with clothes.

get away with	keep up with	smarten up
stand out	dress up	throw on

a I go to at least ten big fashion shows a year, just to .... the latest designs.

b Joan asked me to paint the flat with her, so I .... an old shirt and found my tattiest pair of jeans.

c Henry could .... wearing jeans in his last job, but now he has had to .... himself ....

d Nigel .... for the party, but when he arrived, he really .... , as everyone else was wearing casual clothes.

Reading

4 Look at the photo of a pair of jeans. How old do you think they are? Read the text quickly to find out.

$25,000 may sound excessive for a tatty pair of jeans, but the ones in this picture are not an ordinary pair of Levi's. They are said to be one of the two oldest pairs left. They are certainly the most expensive!

Discovered last year in an old coal mine in Colorado, they were initially sold for $10,000 and then sold on again at a higher price. Then Seth Weisser paid even more for them. Co-owner of a store appropriately called *What Comes Around Goes Around*, he decided to contact Levi's in San Francisco. 'I sent them pictures of the jeans and they were delighted. They would have paid $40,000, I think!'

Levi's has its own museum and Lynn Downey, the company historian, said: 'I knew this would be a treasure that everyone in the company would want us to have, so Levi's agreed to pay one of the highest sums ever for a pair of old jeans.'

Apart from a hole in the left pocket and frayed edges at the bottom, the jeans are in remarkably good condition for their age. Ms Downey was able to date them by their leather patch, which was added in 1886, and the single back pocket. A second pocket was added in 1902. She said: 'Perhaps the most important reason why Levi's bought these jeans is that the company lost everything in the 1906 San Francisco earthquake and the first 50 years of our history was destroyed.'

5 Now read these statements about the text and say whether they are true or false.

   a There are no other jeans as old as these.
   b Seth Weisser paid $10,000 for the jeans.
   c Lynn Downey is an employee of Levi's.
   d The jeans are made completely of one material.
   e The jeans have fewer pockets than ones made after 1902.
   f The Levi's company is more than 100 years old.

6 Underline the four superlative forms in the text.

7 Which words in the text mean:

   a too much ....
   b common ....
   c suitably ....
   d pleased ....
   e worn ....
   f extremely ....

Grammar

Comparatives

8 Make sentences, using a comparative adjective and the other words. An example is given.

   a Cotton shirts/cheap/woollen ones.
     Cotton shirts are cheaper than woollen ones.
   b Flat shoes/comfortable/high-heeled ones.
   c Jeans/casual/trousers.
   d Supermodels/thin/other people.
   e Sarah Thomas/young/Kate Moss.
   f New York/big/San Francisco.
   g Jogging/dangerous/bungee-jumping.
   h Clubbing/tiring/studying.

9 Rewrite these sentences using the structure *not as ... as* and the word in bold.

   a Last year the prices in this shop were lower.
     cheap
     This year the prices in this shop are .... last year.
   b I think this exercise is easy.
     difficult
     This exercise is .... I thought.
   c Ben won the race but George came second.
     fast
     George was .... Ben.

STUDENT'S BOOK **page 198**

FASHION MATTERS 5

2 The virtual world

Reading

1 Skim read this text about two children, Harry and George. Do they prefer computer games or board games?

2 Scan the text for words or phrases that mean the same as a–h.

a enjoy ....

b finding solutions ....

c luck ....

d company ....

e breaking off ....

f enthusiastic ....

g put ....

h restrict ....

Grammar

Present tenses

3 Match the sentence halves a–e and 1–5. Then fill each gap with a suitable verb in the present simple or present continuous.

a A report published this week ....
b Parents .... that many board games
c According to a lot of parents, children .... too much time in front of the TV,
d More and more, parents .... their children from going outside to play
e Board games .... to be particularly attractive,

1 .... educational and social benefits to their children.
2 as they .... the whole family in an enjoyable indoor activity.
3 instead of playing outdoors, which .... that they are less fit nowadays.
4 because they .... it is dangerous.
5 that sales of board games .... at present.

Richard and Vicky Sabotowski try to work hard at their design business, as well as spend time with their two young sons. As games lovers themselves, the couple have found a way to make the most of their time at home. 'We always appreciate playing games as a family,' said Vicky, briefly interrupting an exciting but tense game of *Monopoly*. 'The children – Harry, 5 and George, 9 – really like games such as *Connect 4* and *Guess Who*, which involve working out problems. Because these are games of chance, the cleverest people don't always win – and the children love beating us!'

The children both have computer games, but Vicky believes they find board games more fun. 'We try to limit how often they play on the computer because there's no social interaction. When they do play they get bored easily, but if we suggest a game of something like *Connect 4* they are always keen. To me, computer games are a bit of a cop-out – something to plonk your child in front of while you go and do something else.'

George agreed. 'With computer games you play them on your own and they get really boring. I much prefer playing board games.'

UNIT 2

4 Use suitable verbs from this list in their correct forms to complete the letter. Sometimes, a verb can be used more than once. There is an example at the beginning (0).

forget	hate	keep
know	like	realise
sound	suppose	
understand	wish	

G ···▶ STUDENT'S BOOK **page 198**

Dear Maya

How are you? I (0) ...suppose... you are working hard for your exams at the moment. I (1) .... I am! Although I normally (2) .... to do nothing in the evenings, this week the books are out every night! It's not easy to study, though. My little brother James (3) .... annoying me. He (4) .... I have to study but he (5) .... to be quiet. I (6) .... it most when he plays with his computer games. He (7) .... to turn up the volume and it (8) .... appalling! When I ask him to turn it down he never (9) .... why. Honestly, sometimes I almost (10) .... he wasn't my brother!

Vocabulary

5 Complete this puzzle of words to do with games, by reading the clues below. The number of letters each word has is given in brackets. What word appears vertically?

1 Computer games look great now because they have much better .... than five years ago. (8)
2 A close copy of something. (5)
3 An .... is when you do something exciting. (9)
4 Who you play against. (8)
5 Companies often bring out a newer .... of the same game. (7)
6 You use these when you are fighting. (7)
7 To work out a puzzle or problem. (5)
8 Games usually have very good sound .... (7)

1 _ _ _ _ _ _ _ _
2 _ _ _ _ _
3 _ _ _ _ _ _ _ _ _
4 _ _ _ _ _ _ _ _
5 _ _ _ _ _ _ _
6 _ _ _ _ _ _ _
7 _ _ _ _ _
8 _ _ _ _ _ _ _

6 Choose the right adjective to describe the people in a–e. There is one extra adjective that you do not need to use.

| aggressive | anti-social | demanding |
| mindless | popular | sophisticated |

a Brian turns up the volume on his CD player at 2 am and refuses to turn it down when the neighbours complain.
b Kenny always has several messages on his answerphone when he gets home.
c Victoria is four years old and keeps asking her parents to play with her, even when they are trying to work.
d Judy often gets angry and her boyfriend says she can be violent.
e Claude wears Armani suits and goes to the best nightclubs in town.

7 All the following words occurred in Unit 2. Sort them according to the three headings given. Some can go under more than one heading. Use your dictionary if necessary.

sound effects   interface   upgrade   back-up
graphics   downloading   file   browsing
access (information)   clone   surf the web
submit

The Internet	Computers	Video games

THE VIRTUAL WORLD   **7**

3 Going places

Vocabulary
Prepositions

1 Fill each gap in the story with a suitable preposition.

My favourite place

This has got to be Sipadan, a coral island (1) .... the east coast of Borneo. I stayed (2) .... a little room with just a bed and a wardrobe, nothing (3) .... the walls or floors. It was very simple – everyone ate together (4) .... the terrace (5) .... the front of the building. Just (6) .... the road from the hotel is the beach, which is beautiful. You can walk (7) .... the island in about half an hour, although there are very strict rules about walking (8) .... certain parts of the beach at night because the turtles lay their eggs in the sand. Sipadan has some of the most amazing diving (9) .... the world. You can walk (10) .... the sea and after 200 metres you come (11) .... a coral wall which drops a kilometre straight down (12) .... the ocean floor.

Travel quiz

2 Complete the following sentences with a suitable word. The right number of letters are given to help you.

a I'd really like to go on a _ _ _ _ _ _ round the Greek islands.

b The historic town centre was full of _ _ _ _ _ _ _ _ _ _ with guidebooks and cameras.

c We took the _ _ _ _ _ from Dover to Calais instead of the tunnel.

d When we had a problem on holiday we asked the _ _ _ _ _ _ _ _ .

e I think _ _ _ _ _ _ _ _ are more comfortable than tents.

f My brother was seasick because the _ _ _ _ _ _ _ _ was a bit rough.

g On a ship you sleep in a _ _ _ _ _ _ .

Writing
Phrasal verbs

3 Informal phrasal verbs often have a more formal equivalent. Match one of the phrasal verbs in A with the more formal alternative verb in B.

A	B
1 to **come across** a person	a to be in the mood for
2 to **get over** an illness	b to tolerate
3 to **put up with** a situation	c to manage to see
4 to **ring up** a person	d to leave/depart
5 to **keep on** doing something	e to telephone
6 to **feel like** doing something	f to recover from
7 to **make out** a person/thing	g to meet accidentally
8 to **set off** for a place	h to continue

8 UNIT 3

4 Decide whether these sentences are formal or informal.
   If they are informal, complete them with a phrasal verb from exercise 3.
   If they are formal, complete them with an ordinary verb or expression from exercise 3.

   a I don't always .... making dinner in the evening so I often get a take-away.
   b Coaches .... for Manchester every hour, on a daily basis.
   c I don't know why you .... your brother, he behaves like an idiot.
   d Don't forget to .... Steve to remind him to bring some glasses to the party.
   e We were informed that the company chairman was .... from influenza, and wasn't therefore able to attend the meeting.
   f If you .... to park your car outside my house, I'll have to consider taking legal action.

5 Decide which of the following (a–j) are written and which are spoken forms of English, and whether they are formal or informal.

   Look at this example from the Student's Book:
   You don't have to socialise if you don't want to.
   ANSWER: *Informal, spoken English.*

   a This compartment is reserved for non-smokers. ....
   b John rang, please ring him back sometime tonight. Steve. ....
   c We would be delighted if you could attend our son's wedding on 16th June. ....
   d I wonder if you'd mind very much if I opened the window? ....
   e You must be joking! ....
   f Can I help you, sir? ....
   g Out of order. ....
   h Please give my love to your family. Best wishes, Liz. ....
   i Can you give me a hand with my things? ....
   j Okay, I'll be with you in a second. ....

Grammar
Obligation, necessity, permission

6 Complete the following sentences using a suitable form of the verbs below.

have to	must	need	let	permit

   a In Britain you .... drive on the left.
   b In some countries you .... be 21 in order to drink in a bar.
   c I'm going to stay in bed tomorrow morning as I .... go to work.
   d 'I really think you .... get your hair cut,' said Elizabeth's mother.
   e My sister didn't .... me borrow her clothes when we were teenagers.
   f Peter .... get the bus home last night as the trains were on strike.
   g You .... bought me a new watch for my birthday, my old one works perfectly well.
   h Smoking .... in government offices any more.

   G ···▶ STUDENT'S BOOK page 199

GOING PLACES 9

4 Our four-legged friends

Reading

1 Look at this article about a man, John Franklin, and his wife, Anabel, who are travelling across a very wild part of Canada called the Yukon, on foot.

Before you read, write down:

- the type of problems you think they might encounter
- the animals they might meet
- the likely state of the roads
- where they could sleep.

2 Now read through the article quickly to see if you were right. Don't worry too much at this stage about vocabulary that you don't know.

'Anabel, I think there is a bear in the house,' I shouted up the stairs. She didn't hear me properly. 'There's a what?' she shouted back. 'You've found a chair in the house?' I cleared my throat and said again, as calmly as possible, 'I think there is a bear in the house.' If there is a world speed record for re-packing a rucksack and exiting a building, Anabel must be a contender, for we were outside the building again within seconds, with Anabel giggling at my now idiotic-sounding statement.

Anabel and I had already spent three days walking 80 kilometres over the mountains from the Pacific. We were in Canada's Yukon Territory, heading towards Carcross, on the shore of Lake Bennett. Here our canoe was waiting where we had left it the week before. Our plan then was to canoe down the 3,000 kilometres of the Yukon River to the Bering Sea.

On this day, we were walking the last 48 kilometres towards Carcross, following a disused railway line. Walking along the line was extremely difficult because of the size of the sleepers and the shingle in between. You also need to keep an eye out for black bears, whose presence was evident from the huge piles of dung that littered the tracks.

As the day drew on, we started to look for somewhere to sleep. We finally spotted an old railway building, which looked as if it might keep us safe from prowling bears. It had the name 'Pennington' painted in letters half a metre high on the outside, which is the name of an area in Hampshire, close to where I grew up. Whether there was any connection between the two I have no idea. But it appeared to be a bear-proof spot for the night. Though the windows and doors bore large scratch and chew marks, they were boarded up and looked secure. So, after bending back some of the nails that secured the door bolts, we forced an entry. Anabel went upstairs and started to unpack and settle in while I poked about downstairs.

I was nosing around in what was once clearly a kitchen, when, from out of a darkened doorway that I took to be the larder, came a soft but distinctive deep moan. My curiosity raised, I started to walk towards the slightly open door. I was halfway across the room when a booming growl came out of the darkness. In true comic-book style, the hairs on the back of my neck sprang up. My instinct was to run. I backed out of the room, my eyes glued on the dark doorway. We thought it might be a better idea to spend the night elsewhere and a 45-minute walk down the tracks revealed a small spit of rock pushing into the lake, just large enough for our tent.

We got up early in the morning, keen to walk the remaining kilometres to Carcross. The night's sleep had been adequate, if a little troubled by dreams of bears and things that go 'boo' in the night. But our mood rose with the sun, and by the time the day was properly aired, we were swinging along, relaxing with each step and looking forward to a big lunch at Carcross.

Crossing a small, wooden bridge, we left the rail tracks to have a drink. As we turned, Anabel cried out 'Stop!' Looking up, I saw a familiar black shape behind us: another black bear was following us, creeping up from behind, then disappearing rapidly into the surrounding scrub when we turned to face it. How long it had been shadowing us, we could not say. Suddenly, reaching Carcross as soon as possible seemed like a very good idea.

Guessing unknown words

3 In lines 17–19 of the article it says:

Walking along the [railway] line was extremely difficult because of the size of the sleepers and the shingle in between.

Now you might never have seen *sleepers* and *shingle* before, but you can probably make a guess as to their meaning if you think about what a railway line looks like.

Decide what you think these words from the article mean. There are some clues in brackets to help you.

a heading towards (line 12) ....
b disused (what does *dis* mean?) (line 17) ....
c keep an eye out for (lines 19–20) ....
d littered (what is *litter*?) (line 21) ....
e spotted (line 23) ....
f bear-proof (line 28) ....
g boarded up (what is *a board*?) (line 30) ....
h nosing around (line 34) ....
i the larder (where is this?) (line 36) ....
j glued (what is *glue*?) (line 41) ....

4 Now read the article again more carefully and say whether these statements are true or false.

a Anabel rushed out of the house when she saw the bear. ....
b She thought the incident was very funny. ....
c John and Anabel had started their journey at the coast. ....
d John and Anabel had canoed 3,000 kilometres to Lake Bennett. ....
e They had to keep watch for trains as they were walking. ....
f John had grown up in Pennington. ....
g Bears had been trying to get in the old railway building. ....
h John ran out of the kitchen in fright. ....
i The bear had followed them from the old railway building. ....

5 Look back at the article and find the two examples of 'it' on lines 24 and 55. What does the 'it' refer to in each case?

Grammar
as and *like*

6 Decide whether to use *as* or *like* in the following sentences.

a He can't ride a horse .... well .... I can.
b Susanna prefers activity holidays .... sailing or walking.
c Your sister looks .... you.
d I came to school the same way today .... I did last week.
e He dressed up .... a policeman for the party.
f She used to work in the university .... a zoology lecturer.
g I enjoy going camping when it's warm, ... in July.

Compound adjectives

7 Match the adjectives in the first column with those in the second column.

a duty-   catering
b cross-   free
c long-   handed
d absent-   minded
e hand-   distance
f first-   made
g second-   hand
h self-   class
i right-   eyed

8 Which of the compound adjectives above can be used to describe the following nouns?

a leather bag ....
b journey ....
c car ....
d person ....
e bottle of perfume ....
f ticket ....
g holiday ....

G ⋯⋯ STUDENT'S BOOK **page 199**

5 Fear and loathing

Vocabulary

1 Choose words from the box below to complete this letter of complaint. There are three extra words that you do not need.

next	compensation	disaster
worried	delighted	unhelpful
earlier	dreadful	worse
meant	spend	stiff
refund	thought	conditions
opposite	surprised	impossible

Grammar
Past tenses

2 Complete this table of past tense forms. It includes both regular and irregular verbs from Unit 5.

Infinitive	Past tense	Past participle
find		
flee		
grab		
hold		
keep		
realise		
sink		
swerve		
try		
wave		

Dear Sir

My wife and I took an Ocean Cruise holiday with you last month, which was a (1) .... I am therefore writing to ask for (2) ....

Firstly, the food was (3) .... In fact, my wife fell ill the day after we set off. We believe this was because of the breakfast she had eaten on board (4) .... that day. Her health got (5) .... during the trip but the ship's doctor was very (6) .... I was quite (7) ...., and this ruined the trip for me.

Secondly, our cabin was in an extremely noisy part of the ship, as it was (8) .... the disco. As my wife lay sick in bed, she was (9) .... more than once by drunken dancers who (10) .... our cabin was the nearest toilet. In the end, my wife locked the door. This (11) .... that I could not get into my own cabin late one evening and had to (12) .... the night in the bar.

Last but not least, your brochure promised 'excellent sailing (13) ....'. However, for three days, there was a heavy storm and the ship rolled badly. My wife was scared (14) .... and even I found it unpleasant.

I demand a full (15) .... of the cost of the trip at your earliest convenience.

Yours faithfully

K. Grumpington-Smythe
(Admiral)

3 Fill the gaps using the verbs in brackets in the correct tense.

When Harry (1) .... (see) the cliff ahead of him, he (2) .... (know) that he (3) .... (take) the wrong road. He (4) .... (try) to stop the car but nothing (5) .... (happen). He (6) .... (go) rigid with fear as he (7) .... (realise) that someone (8) .... (interfere) with the brakes ..

Now choose one of these three endings to complete the story. Look up any words you don't understand in your dictionary. Write out the final sentences in full, adding suitable words of your own.

a cliff was getting nearer and nearer/threw himself out of window/car went over cliff
b swerved into field on left/noticed largest pile of hay ever/drove into haystack/survived
c went to pieces/screaming and shouting/car went over cliff/landed two hundred metres below/burst into flames/Harry?

G ⋯→ STUDENT'S BOOK **page 200**

Reading

4 Look at questions 1–8 opposite. Then read the four short texts A–D and answer the questions. Two answers are needed for the last question.

Which text or texts

describes an accident?	1 ___
talks about experiencing fear?	2 ___
mentions a long journey?	3 ___
talks about a camping holiday?	4 ___
is about someone who was alone?	5 ___
talks about something that happened to a relative?	6 ___
describe severe weather?	7 ___ 8 ___

A
A group of us went to Germany two years ago. One afternoon, we had been to a lake to swim and we were strolling back to the tent through the forest. It went quite dark but it wasn't raining. Suddenly there was a flash of light and this enormous tree just to the right in front of us shook violently and started to fall in our direction. We turned and fled in absolute panic. It was a narrow escape. Jenny had dropped her bag. When we went back to find it, it was squashed flat underneath the tree trunk. That could so easily have been us!

B
My friend Mary was on a business trip abroad and she was staying in a luxury hotel. When she had checked in, the people on reception had warned her to lock her door at night, but this particular night she forgot. She says she still remembers waking up in bed and seeing this figure in black standing over her, with all her jewellery in his hands. Thankfully, he hadn't noticed that she was awake, so she closed her eyes again and lay absolutely still, calmly waiting for him to leave. When he did, she phoned the emergency hotel number immediately, but they never caught anyone.

C
It was just before midnight when the doorbell rang. My mother answered and there was a policeman standing there. He said he had some bad news and asked to come in. We took him to the kitchen and sat down. He said that my brother was trapped inside a cave up in Yorkshire with a friend of his. There had been some really heavy rain and the cave was in danger of flooding. He said there was 'little hope' of finding either of them alive. Mum and I didn't sleep all night, waiting for the phone to ring. However, when it did, it was my brother! He said they had found another way out and had spent the last two hours having a really good breakfast.

D
We were driving along this mountain road, miles from anywhere, when we came across a trail of tins of food and bottles of water along the road. I looked out of the car window and noticed this camper van about ten metres below us in a field, with its back door hanging off. It had obviously swerved off the road. We stopped the car. A young man was climbing back up towards the road. He was covered in blood, so we offered to take him to hospital. As we drove off, with him lying on the back seat, he started asking about his girlfriend – was she all right? When we reached the hospital we found that someone else had picked her up and had taken her to casualty. Luckily, she was okay – and so was he, eventually. We went to visit them in hospital the next day. They said they were travelling overland to India.

FEAR AND LOATHING

6 What if?

Reading

1 Read this article about David Ashcroft. What has just happened to him?

A shy cabinet maker* met the press yesterday. It seems his dearest wish after winning £12.3 million on the National Lottery is to buy a new set of tools. At the press conference, 30-year-old David Ashcroft and about 50 journalists looked equally shocked. ☐1

'What's it like to suddenly become the country's most eligible bachelor?'

'I haven't had a chance to give it a thought.'

'Have you got a girlfriend?'

'No.'

'Have you ever had a long-term relationship?'

'No.'

'Aren't you a bit worried some ex-girlfriend is going to come forward?'

'Only if they went back to kindergarten,' said David in a rare flash of humour.

☐2 He had watched in stunned silence as his winning numbers were drawn on TV. Ever since, he has been trying to cope with the news – he has won the seventh largest payout on a single ticket.

The man whose business is restoring furniture told the press he wants to get back to work. ☐3 He held a glass of champagne for the photographers but didn't want any of it because he doesn't drink. 'It was quite a shock,' he said, looking pale.

He remembered Saturday evening well. 'I went into the other room and put on the teletext** and just looked at it for half an hour in disbelief.' ☐4 He didn't tell his parents until the next day, after a sleepless night with his winning ticket under his pillow.

The journalists tried one more line of questioning. 'What car do you drive?'

'I don't drive,' said David, 'but I do have a driving licence and I'll probably get a van.'

This was all too much for the press. 'Don't you want a Porsche?'

'I didn't know they made vans,' said David.

* a person who makes high-quality wooden furniture
** a news and information service available on TV

2 Now choose from the sentences A–E the one which fits each gap (1–4). There is one extra sentence which you do not need to use.

A The multi-millionaire was unwilling to answer their questions.

B Last Saturday, he had sat alone in the small house he shares with his parents.

C Eventually, he phoned his sister Janet, who went round to sit with him for a couple of hours.

D As soon as he has had a holiday with his family, that is.

E Then the journalists got out their notebooks and the questions started to flow.

14 UNIT 6

Grammar

3 Complete these conditional sentences by including the verb in brackets in the correct tense.

a If he .... (buy) a lottery ticket that morning, his life wouldn't have changed.

b Unless someone .... (claim) the prize by 11 pm, the money will be put into the good causes fund.

c Would you talk to the press if they .... (offer) you £10,000?

d If anyone .... (phone), say I'll be back at ten thirty.

e Would you mind if we just .... (grab) a sandwich for lunch?

f If you .... (be) so hard on her, she wouldn't have burst into tears like that.

g I'd give you a lift if my car .... (be) so unreliable.

h I wouldn't be surprised if we .... (end up) in a ditch the way you're driving!

G ⋯⋯⋮ STUDENT'S BOOK **page 200**

4 Put these adverbs of frequency in the correct place in each sentence.

a Lottery winners find it difficult to sleep after they have heard the news. (usually)

b I have time to read long novels these days. (seldom)

c People are telling me to stop working so hard. (always)

d Before the storm, I worried about those trees near the house. (never)

e Now, if it's windy, I'm scared stiff that they'll fall on us. (often)

f What's happened to John? He's here by this time. (normally)

G ⋯⋯⋮ STUDENT'S BOOK **page 200**

5 Complete the second sentence so that it has a similar meaning to the first sentence, using the word given. **Do not change the word given.** You must use between two and five words, including the word given.

1 Unless you leave now, you'll miss the train.
if
You'll miss the train .... now.

2 Helen is often in a panic about her work.
control
Helen is not .... her work.

3 Give me your address, as I might visit Barcelona.
case
Give me your address .... visit Barcelona.

4 I always watch the late night news on TV.
never
I .... the late night news on TV.

5 George didn't get any sleep last night, as usual.
had
Last night, George .... , as usual.

6 Her parents were so shocked they couldn't understand the news.
take
Her parents were so shocked they weren't .... the news.

Vocabulary

6 Look at these sets of words. Which is the odd one out and why? Say what part of speech each set is.

a cheque   account   prize   cash
b gain   give   win   pick up
c shock   delight   panic   confusion
d tense   anxious   suspicious   nervous
e deal with   look after   work out   take off

WHAT IF? **15**

7 Life's too short

Reading

1 Read this article, ignoring the missing sentences for the moment. How did the writer, Victoria Walker, feel after her trip?

Few people have travelled faster on water than they have on land. Even fewer have exceeded 160 km/h in a boat. [1] Holmes took me for a ride in his £100,000 catamaran, *Talley Medical*. He gradually eased *Talley Medical*, which has a six-litre, 600hp engine and can reach 193 km/h, to 169 km/h.

I am a natural panicker, so I was not looking forward to this assignment. [2] There have been several horrifying accidents. Why anyone would want to risk his life, therefore, for the sake of screaming around the ocean at great speed was quite beyond me. I put the question to Holmes. 'I love being on water,' he confessed. 'Once you get salt water in your blood, there's no stopping you.'

The cockpit canopy of *Talley Medical* was made of the same material as a fighter jet. The seats are like a jet's and the space is minimal. [3] I wore full flame-retardant overalls, crash helmet and lifejacket.

Powerboat racing can be an expensive sport. But most people get into the sport at a much lower – and cheaper – level. It is possible to get a second-hand boat that could be used for recreation as well as racing for about £2,000. But it would not be possible simply to buy the top-of-the-range, monster boat if you had, say a big lottery win, then go out racing. [4] Newcomers to the sport have to work their way up through the different races.

It is even possible to make money out of the sport. Holmes has been able to make a good living by using technical expertise as an engineer to build, tune and test boats, as well as winning prize money through his skill as a racer. His skill, however, does not end there. [5] I have had few experiences in my life to equal the thrill and enjoyment I had as we messed about that morning.

2 Read the article again and answer these questions.

a How fast can the catamaran go?
b Why didn't Victoria want to interview Holmes?
c Why was Victoria wearing special clothing?
d Are powerboats only for competitions?
e Can anyone with a powerboat enter a race?

3 What do you think these words in the article mean?

a exceeded ....
b horrifying ....
c the cockpit ....
d flame-retardant ....
e recreation ....

16 UNIT 7

4 Choose from the sentences A–F the one which fits each gap (1–5). There is one extra sentence which you do not need to use.

A Tied in with a five-strap safety harness so tightly I could not move, I was seated behind Holmes in the navigator's chair.
B Instead I tried not to scream as we pulled away.
C But with the help of the five times powerboat world champion, Neil Holmes, I achieved both.
D He proved quite adept at not frightening the life out of me.
E And powerboat racing is dangerous.
F Race organisers would consider it too dangerous for a novice to join a high-power race.

Grammar
Gerunds and infinitives

5 Decide if the following sentences are correct. If not, make the necessary changes.

a Jenny suggested to go to the party in a taxi.
b I look forward to hear from you in the near future.
c I don't mind to do it.
d I'm interested learn Spanish.
e My brother wants to go to Japan.
f I'll help you with your homework when I finish to write my letter.
g I am used to do the washing up.
h Let me make the tea.
i The children were made to get out of bed.
j I'm going to town for buy a new jumper.
k I object to pay to park my car.
l I can't afford to lending you any more money.
m My sister's too small to be a policewoman.

G ⋯▸ STUDENT'S BOOK **page 201**

Vocabulary

6 Complete the following sentences by choosing the correct word.

a I don't think my team will ever (win / beat) the national championships – they are so useless.
b The score at the end of the first half of the football match was 3 – (zero / nil).
c Some football players think the (referee / umpire) is an idiot.
d The basketball team has just had a new (pitch / court) built.
e I got my father a new set of golf (clubs / rackets) for his birthday.
f Most professional tennis players (give / take) up the sport when they reach their mid-thirties.
g The Formula 1 driver completed 30 (lengths / laps) of the track before he had to retire with engine trouble.

Writing

7 Read this story and add the necessary punctuation. You will need to put in CAPITAL LETTERS, full stops (.), commas (,), apostrophes ('), inverted commas (" "), and exclamation marks (!). You must also decide how many paragraphs are needed.

it was the greatest day of my life i had been picked to play for my national football team and now we were playing in the finals of the world cup all of us waited nervously in the changing rooms then all of a sudden it was time we ran through the door and into the tunnel leading to the pitch a wall of noise hit us the fans were all on their feet cheering and shouting i felt so proud the whistle blew and the match began an opportunity came and i took it i could see pele and cantona in the stands shouting go on you can do it so with one great kick i scored a goal all the other players came over to congratulate me and hug me i heard them saying come on its time to wake up it was a woman's voice i didn't know there were any women in our team I said to myself and at that moment i woke up and heard my doctor telling me I would make a full recovery

8 Write a story which ends with these words.

We all enjoyed playing, even though we didn't win.

Write 120–180 words in all.

Things to think about
- What sport are you going to write about?
- Do you need any special vocabulary?
- Are you a player or spectator?
- Where was the match being held?
- Was it an important game or one at college?
- How did you feel at the beginning, in the middle and at the end?
- Did anything special happen during the match?
- Remember to punctuate your story!

LIFE'S TOO SHORT 17

8 Downshifting

Vocabulary

1 Find the twelve words for jobs and professions in this wordsearch. Words can be horizontal, vertical or diagonal. They may run forwards or backwards.

  a a person who designs houses
  b a person who steals from banks
  c a doctor who specialises in mental problems
  d a person who walks down a cat-walk
  e a person who works in a bank
  f a person who puts in your central heating
  g a person who is in charge of a school
  h a person who cuts people open in hospital
  i a person who looks after you on holiday
  j a person in charge of a ship
  k an animal doctor
  l a person who works in a prison

2 Use a dictionary to find out the difference between these pairs of words or expressions.

  a to be made redundant / to get the sack
  b to do shift-work / to do flexi-time
  c a trade / a profession
  d an employer / an employee
  e to be unemployed / to be on maternity leave
  f to do overtime / to put in for a rise

R	O	T	C	A	S	H	I	E	R	A	E	T	L
S	S	B	D	T	M	E	D	M	B	C	Y	E	E
S	W	R	V	O	N	A	R	D	M	O	P	V	R
I	A	E	R	K	A	D	T	C	F	I	H	O	M
R	T	I	I	X	M	M	O	D	E	L	D	S	M
T	P	R	E	D	W	A	R	D	E	R	S	K	R
A	G	U	R	L	K	P	S	A	G	H	T	E	O
I	A	O	C	A	P	T	A	I	N	K	B	M	B
H	V	C	N	M	E	J	W	F	U	M	Q	U	B
C	E	X	N	C	D	Z	F	C	U	Q	E	N	E
Y	O	R	E	D	R	O	B	L	P	O	R	O	R
S	U	R	G	E	O	N	P	H	W	M	Z	N	C
P	S	Y	A	R	C	H	I	T	E	C	T	A	T

3 Complete the following sentences with an appropriate word or expression from exercise 2.

  a My next door neighbour .... for always arriving late.
  b Peter's dad is a dentist and he wants to take up the same ....
  c I really need the money so I'm going to .... even if I have no time left to see my friends.
  d My boss is a really helpful ....
  e I'm much happier now I do .... It means I can suit myself when I get to work.
  f Mr Jones has been .... for the past six months.

UNIT 8

4   Read the text below and decide which answer (A, B, C or D) best fits each gap.

Gestures that give you away

Scratching your nose during a (1) .... interview can have a real impact on your chances (2) .... success. That's the finding of body language expert Stephen Field, who has warned of the importance of certain gestures and phrases when being interviewed. He says that people who have a sudden (3) .... in nervous hand-to-face contact, such as nose scratching, are probably lying. And if they start sentences with phrases like 'to (4) .... the truth' or 'to be perfectly honest', they are almost certainly lying. Mr Field is convinced that women are more aware of these (5) .... signals than men because of a difference in brain structure. (6) .... less than 15 per cent of men are able to read non-verbal signals. If a man is going to lie to a woman and doesn't want to be (7) .... out, he is better off doing it by fax or phone (8) .... she can't see him. Mr Field says that jobseekers (9) .... be very careful about the non-verbal signals that they send out. He also says that interviewers must try not to (10) .... a decision on whether to employ the person or not in the first 60 seconds.

1   A work   3   A growth   5   A unchangeable   7   A caught   9   A have
    B post   B increase   B unconscious   B make   B ought
    C position   C raise   C uncomfortable   C got   C used
    D job   D gain   D unconvincing   D had   D should
2   A for   4   A tell   6   A Clearly   8   A while   10   A come
    B of   B say   B Obviously   B whereas   B find
    C on   C speak   C Apparently   C so   C conclude
    D from   D talk   D Surely   D therefore   D make

Grammar

used to and would

5   Read through the following article and decide which of the following would be suitable – *used to*, *would* or the past simple tense. There is sometimes more than one possibility.

 STUDENT'S BOOK **page 201**

New research shows that the introduction of labour-saving gadgets has meant that men and women take a third less exercise today than they (1) .... (do) a generation ago. Scientists (2) .... (find) that practically every sphere of life has been influenced by the development of labour-saving devices which have conspired to make us put on weight. They (3) .... (discover) that using a cordless phone at home cut down walking in the home by 10 miles a year. Other comparative indicators (4) .... (include) the amount of energy used in making a bed with a duvet and one with blankets and sheets. A housewife in the 1950s (5) .... (spend) about two hours a week and (6) .... (use) up 300 calories more than a person does nowadays.

Ernest Shaw, 69, (7) .... (confirm) how hard it (8) .... (be) to run a home in the 1950s. 'The jobs (9) .... (take) much more effort. The nearest shops (10) .... (be) a quarter of a mile away and my wife (11) .... (walk) there and back, carrying the shopping in heavy bags. There (12) .... (be) no supermarkets. You (13) .... (visit) the greengrocer, the dairy and the butcher.' The scientists (14) .... (estimate) that a shopper in the 1950s would have spent about 10 hours and 2,300 calories a week walking from shop to shop.

DOWNSHIFTING 19

9 The hard sell

Reading

1 Read the article below, ignoring the missing sentences. How is the food industry failing shoppers?

What do they really mean?

Food manufacturers and retailers are letting shoppers down. This is the view of the CWS, which has just brought out a new report.

According to the report, shoppers believe food labels because they think there are strict regulations in place. **1** ☐ So the food industry can get away with all sorts of cunning strategies to make products look bigger and sound better than they are.

The report has identified the different ways in which shoppers are misled. **2** ☐ Descriptions on packaging are sometimes inaccurate in an attempt to oversell the product. One example given in the report is the phrase 'haddock fillets', used for a product that is in fact cut from big blocks of fish rather than individual fillets.

3 ☐ These include 'traditional', 'wholesome', or 'premium'. The claim that a brand is '90% fat-free' hides the fact that it contains 10% fat, which is above recommended levels. Phrases such as 'free from preservatives' make a virtue out of a normal attribute of food.

Labels have a wide variety of text sizes on them. You sometimes need a magnifying glass to read the small print. **4** ☐

Another deliberate type of misinformation lies in the image. Many pictures on packets use small plates to make the product look bigger. **5** ☐

However, misleading messages on packaging could soon be a thing of the past. The CWS* recently produced a code** which, if used, would end the current inaccuracies and half truths. **6** ☐ The minister for consumer affairs says the code 'will receive very serious consideration'.

* Co-operative Wholesale Society
** a set of rules

2 Choose from sentences A–G the one which fits each gap (1–6). There is one extra sentence which you do not need to use.

A Meaningless adjectives are often used to give a positive message.

B It has called on the government to support it, as a way of improving food standards.

C This verdict has not pleased the food industry.

D By contrast, the hard sell information is given emphasis.

E The rules are, in reality, very weak at present.

F Photographs are sometimes retouched to achieve the same effect.

G The most common of these is poor labelling.

3 Find these words in the gapped article or sentences A–G.

a four nouns to do with law
b three phrasal verbs

20 UNIT 9

Grammar
Modals

4 Complete the sentences with *must*, *might* or *could* (both are possible), *can't* or *couldn't* (both are possible).

a This .... possibly be the new Coca-Cola advert, though why on earth are they using polar bears?

b The ad for the Pentium chip .... be the best of the year – the way they manage to make a computer chip appear interesting is inspired!

c Here's an ad that shows a picture of thirty different puddings – it .... just be advertising desserts, surely?

d Do you remember that ad for a fizzy drink? It .... have been very successful, as they had to withdraw it almost immediately.

e Those ads for Mac computers .... be very successful. They've had so many hits on the Internet!

f Product placement on TV shows .... be more effective than actual commercials – it depends on how many people are watching at the time, I suppose.

G ···▶ STUDENT'S BOOK **page 201**

Vocabulary

6 With which of these words and phrases can you use the adjective *broad*? Which adjective goes with the remaining words and phrases? When you have decided, use a dictionary to study the different uses of this adjective and *broad*.

a range of beliefs
b avenue of trees
c sigh
d Scottish accent
e smile of welcome
f feeling of suspicion
g choice
h breath

5 Read this text and think of the word which best fits each gap. Use only one word in each gap. There is an example at the beginning (0).

GIRL POWER SETS NEW MOOD FOR ADVERTS

More and (0) ......*more*...... advertisements are using strong images of women (1) .... sell products and (2) .... seems that certain members of (3) .... public are upset by them. Three separate adverts, for Lee Jeans, Wallis Clothes and the Nissan Micra car, (4) .... criticised as sexist and tasteless. Some people went further, saying the adverts would possibly encourage violence. However, the Advertising Standards Authority, in (5) .... of receiving nearly 100 complaints about the three adverts, decided that they do (6) .... cause serious offence. The advertising industry (7) .... pleased with the ASA's decision and argues that advertisers (8) .... be right in getting away from the traditional 'washing up and cleaning' role of women. 'Women play (9) .... more active role in society today. We are just reflecting (10) .... ,' said Howard Roberts, planning director of the agency (11) .... produced the 'Ask before you borrow it' Nissan Micra campaign. Although this type of advertising (12) .... be just a 'passing fad', the ASA itself believes that girl power has completely changed the relationship between men and women in advertising.

7 Complete these definitions with words about advertising.

a A .... is a short song or tune used in TV commercials.

b A .... is a short phrase about a product that is easy to remember.

c The .... for a project is the amount of money available for it.

d If something makes an .... on you, it has a powerful effect.

e A .... is a type of product made by a particular company.

THE HARD SELL 21

10 The final frontier

Vocabulary

1 For questions 1–12, read the article below and decide which answer (A, B, C or D) best fits each gap. There is an example at the beginning (0).

Example:
0 A in B on C at D by

Answer: A

New hunt for life in space

British space scientists are planning to join the Americans (0) ..... the race to find evidence of life on other planets. Alan Penny and his team at the Rutherford Appleton Laboratory have (1) ..... a telescope that is 40 times more (2) ..... than Hubble. (3) ..... as 'Darwin', this telescope could tell if planets 50 light years away have any (4) ..... of life on them. Two days after NASA scientists had shown proof that one of Jupiter's moons could support life, Penny (5) ..... that his telescope may be included in a European Space Agency mission. The Darwin project, with a (6) ..... of £500 million, is on a shortlist of two proposals. If approved, it will probably be (7) ..... in around five years' time, its destination somewhere between Mars and Jupiter. The blueprint is actually for five telescopes positioned 50 metres (8) ..... in space, slowly circling a central processing station. The combined data from these telescopes would (9) ..... a full picture of a planet, picking out faint images that have never been seen before. Darwin would not be able to take detailed photographs of the planets it (10) ..... , but Penny believes a second-generation telescope could be sent up to do this. He claims it is worthwhile mapping the universe around our own galaxy, even though these planets lie (11) ..... our reach for the moment. The European Space Agency is expected to make a (12) ..... shortly on whether the Darwin project will go ahead.

1	A thought	B intended	C designed	D drawn
2	A striking	B powerful	C forceful	D strong
3	A Known	B Called	C Considered	D Named
4	A shape	B race	C brand	D kind
5	A announced	B spoke	C advertised	D told
6	A price	B schedule	C charge	D budget
7	A driven	B fetched	C launched	D taken
8	A apart	B far	C distant	D away
9	A save up	B end up	C build up	D put up
10	A invents	B searches	C discovers	D looks
11	A out	B toward	C beyond	D over
12	A conclusion	B decision	C verdict	D view

UNIT 10

Phrasal verbs

2 Match the phrasal verbs below to the definitions a–f.
   Then use these phrasal verbs in a suitable tense to complete sentences 1–6.

   | get on | take off | end up | set up | turn out | run out |

   a leave the ground   b produce   c make progress
   d make arrangements for   e finish   f have no more left

   1 NASA's Galileo spacecraft finally went into orbit around Jupiter in December 1995; the rocket carrying Galileo .... from Earth in 1991.

   2 A leading professor predicts that humans .... with enormous heads to hold their genetically-improved brains.

   3 Factories around the world .... more and more goods that we don't really need.

   4 If customers keep ordering the chocolate cake, we .... by lunchtime!

   5 A series of public lectures .... next year by the university.

   6 How .... with that astronomy course you're doing?

Grammar
Future tenses

3 Make predictions about the future using these notes. Use the range of future structures covered in Unit 10. An example is given.

   near future/scientists/work on moon.
   In the near future, scientists will be working on the moon.

   a 20 years/manned spacecraft/land on Mars.
   ....

   b 22nd century/launch starships/destination/other galaxies.
   ....

   c Soon/people travel to low orbit/Europe to New Zealand only an hour.
   ....

   Now write three more predictions of your own.
   ....
   ....
   ....

4 Read the advert below. Write a paragraph on this forthcoming event, using suitable future tenses and other words from this unit.

   SPACE: THE FUTURE

   Conference at Elwood College of Technology, Melbourne, Australia
   10-12 January 2012
   Guest speakers:
   ○ science fiction writer John T. Price
   ○ leading scientist Prof Paul Rhodes
   Topics for discussion include:
   beam-up technology
   moon settlements
   how to contact aliens

   G ⋯⋯ STUDENT'S BOOK **page 202**

11 Like mother, like daughter

Vocabulary

1 Read this short article. Then use each word given in capitals to form a word that fits in the numbered gap. There is an example at the beginning (0).

How to find a partner

So you want to find a partner? Well, (0) ....*sincerity*.... (SINCERE) is the best policy – be yourself. And if you meet someone who resembles you, physically or (1) .... (MENTAL), then all the better. 'Simply put, opposites don't attract, but similar types do,' says Dr Robin Russell of London University, who has spent a decade studying patterns of (2) .... (ATTRACT). 'On average, the more similar you are to your partner in every way, from (3) .... (PERSON) and attitudes to (4) .... (APPEAR) and obscure physiological factors like elbow shape, the more you're (5) .... (LIKE) to get on.'

There are any number of theories why. Early life might programme you to seek partners who resemble your parents – and by (6) .... (EXTEND) resemble you. Or (7) .... (POSSIBLE) you make a random (8) .... (CHOOSE), but within your (9) .... (SOCIETY) environment there's a more than (10) .... (REASON) chance you will choose people who resemble you than not.

2 Put these adjectives describing personality into order of strength. If you think some are the same strength, put them together.

EXAMPLE: *(weak)* upset   irritated   angry   furious *(strong)*

a petrified	afraid	terrified	nervous
b thrilled	delighted	overjoyed	pleased
c depressed	disappointed	miserable	unhappy
d interested	obsessed	fascinated	keen
e speechless	surprised	astonished	incredulous
f beautiful	attractive	stunning	lovely
g ugly	revolting	unattractive	plain

American English

3 In Unit 11 of the Student's Book, the interview is with an American called Hannah. She uses these words and phrases which are American English:

I guess I was pretty privileged ...
I just loved ...
On the subway ...
She got real embarrassed ...

How would an English person say the phrases above?

4 Look at these other examples of American English and match them with the British English equivalents.

American English	British English
1 first floor	a sellotape
2 Fall	b motorway
3 cookie	c lift
4 trunk	d bank note
5 vacation	e petrol
6 freeway	f Autumn
7 gasoline	g ground floor
8 apartment	h flat
9 Scotch tape	i boot (of a car)
10 elevator	j holiday
11 bill	k biscuit

Writing

5 Read through this letter to a friend and correct it. There are twenty grammatical or spelling errors in the letter.

> Dear Jody,
> Thanks for your letter; it was good to here from you. You'll be pleased knowing that I've found someone to shair the flat with. She's called Elena Richmann and she's actress from Canada. I interviewed about 20 people before I seen her. She's very nicely and we really get on well together. Let me say you a bit about her. She's about 1m 52cm in hieght and has short, black, curly hair; in fact she look a bit like your sister! She's incredibly alive so she should be fun to have around. We're both interested at the same type of films and we seem to have similar tastes of music. She hates cook so I won't have to worrying about having a messy kitchen!
>
> One drawback is that, when she has making a movie, she needs getting up really early, about 4.30 in the morning, to go to the set to get her make-up and costume sorted out. She says she'll be really quite, so we'll have to see. Anyway, I haven't noticed of any bad habits yet! You must to meet her — why don't you come over to the flat next Saterday and we can have a meal together? Drop me a line to let me know.
> Love
> Tanya

6 Look at these photos. B is a photo of your old neighbours and A is a photo of the people who have just moved in next door.

A

B

Now, write a letter to a friend of between 120–180 words telling him/her about the new neighbours. Compare them with the old neighbours you used to have and say which ones you prefer.
You do not need to include postal addresses.

LIKE MOTHER, LIKE DAUGHTER

12 A great idea

Reading

1 For questions 1–7, choose the answer (A, B, C or D) which you think fits best according to the text.

Science flying in the face of gravity

It looked just like another aircraft from the outside. The pilot told his young passengers that it was built in 1964, a Boeing KC-135 refuelling tanker, based on the 707. But appearances were deceptive, and the 13 students from Europe and the USA who boarded the aircraft were in for the flight of their lives.

Inside, the area that normally had seats had become a long white tunnel. Heavily padded from floor to ceiling, it looked a bit like a lunatic asylum. There were almost no windows, but lights along the padded walls eerily illuminated it. Most of the seats had been taken out, apart from a few at the back, where the young scientists quickly took their places with a look of apprehension.

For 12 months, science students from across the continents had competed to win a place on the flight at the invitation of the European Space Agency. The challenge had been to suggest imaginative experiments to be conducted in weightless conditions.

For the next two hours the Boeing's flight resembled that of an enormous bird which had lost its reason, shooting upwards towards the heavens before hurtling towards Earth. The intention was to achieve weightlessness for a few seconds.

The aircraft took off smoothly enough, but any feelings that I and the young scientists had that we were on anything like a scheduled passenger service were quickly dismissed when the pilot put the plane into a 45-degree climb which lasted around 20 seconds. Then the engines cut out and we became weightless. Everything became confused and left or right, up or down no longer had any meaning. After ten seconds of free-fall descent the pilot pulled the aircraft out of its nosedive. The return of gravity was less immediate than its loss, but was still sudden enough to ensure that some students came down with a bump.

Each time the pilot cut the engines and we became weightless, a new team conducted its experiment. First it was the Dutch who wanted to discover how it is that cats always land on their feet. Then the German team, who conducted a successful experiment on a traditional building method to see if it could be used for building a future space station. The Americans had an idea to create solar sails that could be used by satellites.

After two hours of going up and down in the plane doing their experiments, the predominant feeling was one of exhilaration rather than nausea. Most of the students thought it was an unforgettable experience and one they would be keen to repeat.

1 What does the writer say about the plane?

 A It had no seats.
 B The inside was painted white.
 C It had no windows.
 D The outside was misleading.

2 What does 'eerily' on line 14 mean?

 A clearly   B badly   C strangely   D brightly

3 According to the writer, how did the young scientists feel at the beginning of the flight?

 A sick   B nervous   C keen   D impatient

4 What did the pilot do with the plane?

 A He quickly climbed and then stopped the engines.
 B He climbed and then made the plane fall slowly.
 C He took off normally and then cut the engines for 20 seconds.
 D He climbed and then made the plane turn over.

5 What was the point of being weightless?

 A To see what conditions are like in space.
 B To prepare the young scientists for future work in space.
 C To show the judges of the competition what they could do.
 D To allow the teams to try out their ideas.

6 What does 'it' on line 61 refer to?

 A the exhilaration
 B the trip
 C the plane
 D the opportunity

7 Why was this text written?

 A To encourage young people to take up science.
 B To show scientists what young people can do.
 C To report on a new scientific technique.
 D To describe the outcome of a scientific competition.

26 UNIT 12

Grammar

2 The *Cambridge Learner Corpus* shows us that FCE candidates often make mistakes with the passive. Correct these sentences.

a I had to been train by the manager.
b Usually cuckoo clocks make out of wood.
c The science exhibition will be visit by many people.
d My camera stolen on the bus.
e He was stolen his bike.
f It has been prove that water freezes at 0 degrees C.
g One speaks French here.
h Many designs have make for new planes.
i The house is painting at the moment.
j The car cleaned.
k Maria born in April.
l A jet flies by Hamid every day.
m They were asking to a party.
n Today's meeting has cancelled.
o My house was building last year.
p I hurt in a road accident.

Vocabulary

3 Read through this short article about Coca-Cola and decide which answer (A, B, C or D) best fits each gap.

The first glasses of Coca-Cola were drunk in 1886. The drink was first (1) …… by a US chemist called John Pemberton. It was invented at a (2) …… when healthy, non-alcoholic drinks were (3) …… favour in many parts of the USA. Only special bars, called Soda Fountains, sold Coke, (4) …… it was never bottled. This changed in 1922. It was this, plus a (5) …… advertising campaign that made Coca-Cola a world name. Today half a billion Cokes are sold every day in 180 countries. Yet its first (6) …… in 1886 was only 'drink this – it's refreshing'.

1 A formed   B done   C found   D made
2 A time   B season   C date   D year
3 A on   B at   C in   D with
4 A although B since   C unless   D if
5 A heavy   B strong   C deep   D high
6 A slogan   B motto   C jingle   D phrase

Phrasal verbs with *come* and *take*

4 Look at the context of these phrasal verbs and decide on their meaning. Try not to use a dictionary until you have finished the exercise.

a He **came into** a lot of money when his grandfather died.
b She certainly **takes after** her mother – she's so tall.
c He **took up** golf when he retired.
d It took him two hours to **come round** after the blow to his head.
e I'll be **taking over** the business when my father retires.
f It was a problem we rarely **come up against**.
g I didn't **take to** him at first, but now he's one of my best friends.
h The Prime Minister didn't **come up with** any new ideas for tackling crime.
i The information was too much to **take in** at first.
j I **came across** an old letter in the attic the other day.
k Her new job means that she will be **taking on** more responsibility.

A GREAT IDEA 27

13 Education for life

Reading

1 Below is an article about a teacher called Chris Searle. Read the first paragraph to find out more about him. Then skim the skeleton text for general meaning. Ignore the missing sentences for the moment.

Stepney Words

Chris Searle started teaching at Sir John Cass Secondary School in Stepney, East London, in 1970. This particular job had appealed to him partly because he knew the area. More importantly, he had done his postgraduate thesis on an East End poet, Isaac Rosenberg, and saw this part of London as 'a very poetical place'.

Searle had only just qualified but certain progressive ideas about education were already settling in his head. **1** Some of the governors and teachers were ex-army or had a church background; gowns were worn and canes were used to punish trouble-makers if necessary. Stepney was a poor area and the rest of the staff saw no hope for their pupils. However, to Chris Searle, these under-achieving teenagers were the 'sons and daughters of the poet Rosenberg' and poetry was the key that would unlock their potential.

2 The short verses they wrote were sad and often bitter, with the East End shown as a place of no hope. To some of the staff at Sir John Cass, Searle's approach was alarming. Here was a teacher in his early twenties using the school as a laboratory for radical theories of education, and encouraging pupils to speak out. His classroom was noisy and lots of the girls had crushes on him. He saw pupils after school too, as he ran a half-price film club and lived in Stepney, unlike most of his fellow-teachers, who fled each night to the suburbs.

Despite the negative attitudes of colleagues, Searle continued to focus on poetry. He persuaded a photographer, Ron McCormick, to bring his portraits of East London into class and with these visual images, the poems got better and better. **3** The school governors, who thought these poems were too 'gloomy', had ordered Searle not to go ahead with the collection, but by March 1971, *Stepney Words* was out, paid for by Searle and parents. Extracts were even printed in the Sun newspaper.

Searle's 'enemies' (his own word) now made their move. One lunchtime in late May, the head called Searle in and fired him, instructing him not to come in after the end of the month. **4** Zeinaida de la Cruz, a strong-willed 16-year-old girl from Gibraltar, took charge: 'We arranged for people to tell each class. Immediately, everyone wanted to take action.'

When asked recently why they had all taken such a strong line on the sacking, she explained: 'It just didn't seem fair that a teacher everyone liked was being thrown out.' She remembers walking into the offices of a local newspaper after school to tell them what was going on. **5** Searle walked nervously to the school the next morning and found some 800 children standing outside the gates in the rain, where they stayed all day. Thanks to Zeinaida, the journalists came along too. There was also a sympathy walk-out by the cleaning ladies, who made their feelings known by refusing to wipe the 'Don't sack Searle' graffiti off the school walls.

Other schools joined in and the next day there was a march to Trafalgar Square, in the centre of London. Searle stayed away, not wanting to be seen as their leader, but he did not let the matter rest from then on. **6** He also fought his dismissal through the union. In May 1973, the government education secretary, Margaret Thatcher, ruled that Searle should be reinstated at the school. However, ignored by other staff and denied a class of his own, he decided to leave the school for good in July 1974. Searle has continued to teach, however, and has worked in many different countries around the world. He has also published his own poetry.

Lock up, unlock
That's me job for now
Lock up in the morning
Unlock at the end of day

It's an easy life
This job is
Just unlock in the morning
Enjoy meself all day

But at night, me back
It starts hurting
I can't bend
And turn that key

This job at night
It's not for me
In the daytime it's alright
But it's hard to turn
The key at night.

Christine Garratt

UNIT 13

2 Now choose from sentences A–G the one which fits each gap (1–6). There is one extra sentence which you do not need to use.

A His class heard the news the same afternoon.

B However, many pupils had seen their own parents on strike picket lines, so they did.

C Searle contacted a local printer to arrange for their publication.

D They called the national press, which transformed the protest into a major event.

E These views were not shared by the school, which, although quite new, was run very traditionally.

F Although banned from the school, he managed to publish a second *Stepney Words* later that year.

G So he made them read it and write it, believing that in this way, his pupils would make sense of their lives and their surroundings.

Grammar
Reported speech

3 Here are some quotes from Chris Searle and his pupils, who were featured in a radio programme about *Stepney Words*. Rewrite them as reported speech. The first one is started for you.

a I went to the local paper and told them our plans. They asked me some questions to check me out, but in the end they promised to run the story. (Zeinaida)
Zeinaida said that she had gone to the local paper ...

b That morning I went in through the side entrance. The school secretary was handing out the registers as normal, but there can't have been more than 20 or 30 kids in the whole building. (Chris Searle)

c While we were outside the gates, teachers came across and talked to us. Some were sympathetic, though they weren't able to admit it. Some were aggressive and threw gym shoes at us! (a pupil)

d Those children were made to feel that being ordinary meant failure. But it is the ordinary people and their daily work that make a country. (Chris Searle)

G ⇢ STUDENT'S BOOK **page 203**

Vocabulary

4 What do 'trouble-makers' do? There are three other expressions with *make* in the article. Find them and look up their meanings in a dictionary. Then use the expressions and two of the ones below to complete this short text about Chris Searle.

| make a start   make a good impression   make use of |

Chris Searle (1) .... on his pupils, because he helped them to (2) .... how they lived. To publish *Stepney Words*, he (3) .... a local printer. The school governors did not approve of the book and soon after it came out, they (4) .... and had him dismissed. Although Searle eventually got his job back at the school, the other teachers there (5) .... to him and in the end, he chose to leave the school.

5 In these sentences written by FCE candidates, use either a form of *make* or another verb collocation to fill the gaps.

a Our school is going to .... improvements to its reception area.
b I .... a very bad experience with tents while I was camping last year.
c Paul .... up his mind to propose marriage to Mary.
d Finally, could you .... me a favour?
e Technology has .... my life easier.
f I don't need to .... a diet or spend money in a gym.
g I believe that all parents should .... the first step to .... their children aware of the problems.
h Cycling is one of the best ways to .... exercise.
i I really .... myself at home.
j Saying goodbye always .... me cry.

EDUCATION FOR LIFE 29

14 Career moves

Grammar

1 For questions 1–12, read the text and think of the word which best fits each gap. Use only one word in each gap. There is an example at the beginning (0).

Walt Disney had done a number of jobs (0) ......*before*...... he entered the film industry. His first job (1) .... 1917 was on the railroad. Because he claimed to (2) .... sixteen they took him on, although in reality he was (3) .... year younger. He was given (4) .... company's standard blue uniform (5) .... gold buttons and told that (6) .... job was to collect baskets full of fruit, peanuts, chocolate bars and soft drinks from Kansas City station and try to sell as (7) .... as possible on the trains. The first trip he (8) .... was to end in disaster. Half-way (9) .... an eight-hour journey to Jefferson City he had already sold (10) .... of drink and had left all the empty bottles in an end carriage. But (11) .... he returned for them, he discovered that the carriage had gone. The conductor explained that it had (12) .... detached at a station along the route, as it always was. This was an unfortunate start for Walt!

Writing

2 Read this first sentence of a story about a young millionaire. Then reorder sentences a–i to complete the story. Looking at the tenses used will help you to decide on the correct order.

As a child, Tom Gardiner had always known that he would be rich.

a For instance, many customers have had to return faulty software.

b This year, it had been expected that Tom's company would perform even better.

c There have also been reports of a strange virus in some products, which causes a computer screen to go orange and then flash up the message 'Tom is sinking'.

d When the company made record profits last June, Tom celebrated in style, by throwing a huge party on board his magnificent yacht.

e Even if the company survives, Tom has been given a clear warning, which he cannot afford to ignore.

f It seems that one particularly discontented employee has attempted to programme bankruptcy for Tom's company.

g The whole event cost nearly a million pounds, with the bill for flowers alone equivalent to the yearly salary of one of his programmers.

h At 19, he had set up his own software company, and it soon took off in a big way.

i But recently, unimaginable things have been going wrong.

3 Write another 50 words, continuing the story about Tom and ending with this sentence.
Tom's life as an idle millionaire has come to an end.

UNIT 14

Vocabulary

4 Read the text below. Use the word given in capitals at the end of some of the lines to form a word that fits in the gap in the same line. There is an example at the beginning (0).

Tile Art

Just imagine relaxing in your bath (0) ...*surrounded*... by a tropical beach scene. Or working in the kitchen alongside a wonderful (1) .... of hand-painted fruits. These are just two examples of the beautiful (2) .... designed wall tiles that Jan and Barry Harmer (3) .... in. The Harmers have been very (4) .... with their company, *Tile Art*, which they started two years ago. 'There was limited (5) .... of good-quality English tiles,' explains Barry. 'We both felt this was an (6) .... area that we could explore together.' Their designs are very (7) .... and they have had some (8) .... orders. One man turned up with a picture of a JCB (9) .... machine, wanting a mural of himself in the driver's seat holding his new-born baby. The Harmers clearly enjoy running their small business from home and say they have no plans for (10) ....

SURROUND
SELECT
INDIVIDUAL
SPECIAL
SUCCESS
AVAILABLE
DEVELOP
IMAGINE
USUAL
DIG
EXPAND

5 Look at the phrases with *all* below. The first three came up in the Student's Book, but what do the others mean? Use a dictionary to find out if necessary. Then use the phrases to complete sentences a–f.

| of all | for all | all in all |
| all in | after all | all very well |

a I've been very happy working here, ...
b It's .... for the directors to make us travel on cheap, late-night flights, but I doubt if they would do so.
c People who work from home often claim that flexibility is the biggest benefit ....
d Our department is quite productive, ... the office discontent.
e Because of an unexpected order, the company announced that there would be no redundancies ....
f After his long night-shift, he looked ....

6 These words from the Student's Book are all to do with money.

overheads	salary	revenue	redundancy
grant	earnings	income	profits
takings	wages	unemployment benefit	

Some relate to both people and companies. For example, you can say:

The company reduced its overheads to save money. My main overheads are the monthly payments on the house and the car.

Decide how the other words can be used, dividing them into these groups.

Both	Only of people	Only of companies
overheads		

CAREER MOVES   31

15 Too many people?

Vocabulary

1 Read this article about the environmental group Greenpeace and decide which answer (A, B, C or D) best fits each gap. There is an example at the beginning (0).

Example:
0 A protect   B care   C look   D tend
Answer: A

GREENPEACE

Greenpeace is an independent organisation that campaigns to (0) ..... the environment. It has approximately 4.5 million members worldwide in 158 countries, 300,000 of these in the United Kingdom. (1) ..... in North America in 1971, it has since opened offices round the world. As (2) ..... as its campaigning (3) ..... , it also has a charitable trust which (4) ..... scientific research and (5) ..... educational projects on environmental issues. Greenpeace (6) ..... in non-violent direct action. Activists (7) ..... public attention to serious threats to the environment. (8) ..... issues on which the organisation is campaigning include the atmosphere (global warming), the (9) ..... of the rainforests and toxic (10) ..... being emitted from factories.

1	A Built	B Formed	C Invented	D Produced
2	A long	B far	C good	D well
3	A work	B job	C occupation	D position
4	A pays	B funds	C rewards	D earns
5	A undertakes	B engages	C commits	D enters
6	A accepts	B depends	C holds	D believes
7	A draw	B pay	C get	D take
8	A Recent	B Current	C Immediate	D Next
9	A ruin	B extinction	C destruction	D downfall
10	A waste	B litter	C rubbish	D leftovers

2 Complete the spaces to make a word you have used in the Student's Book. To help you, the number of spaces is correct.

a People put used glass and paper in separate containers so they can be _ _ _ _ _ _ _ _ _ _ .

b The dinosaurs are an _ _ _ _ _ _ _ _ species.

c I can't afford a new car, I'll have to get a _ _ _ _ _ _ - _ _ _ _ one.

d Last year there was a _ _ _ _ _ _ _ _ because there wasn't enough water.

e This year there are _ _ _ _ _ _ _ because there has been too much rain.

f A _ _ _ _ _ _ of lightning lit up the sky, and then came the thunder.

g We got caught in a heavy _ _ _ _ _ _ _ and didn't have an umbrella with us.

UNIT 15

Writing

3 You have recently had a letter from your penfriend, Susan, telling you about the area where she lives in Scotland. Read through the letter and decide which of the words below best fits each gap.

> although   as a result   so   besides
> though   when   furthermore
> despite   as   because

4 Now write your reply to Susan. Remember to use your English-English dictionary if necessary.

Think about:
- Location: in the north of, to the south of
- Size: an average-sized town, a small village, the capital city
- Climate: damp, humid, tropical, temperate, arid
- Landscape: mountainous, flat, hilly, forested, built-up
- Population activity: agricultural, industrial, academic, fishing

Dear ....,

It was great to hear from you last week and to get all your news. We're all fine here and looking forward to the summer holidays. I thought in this letter that I'd tell you a little bit about Dunlochry, where I live.

(1) .... you know, I live in a very quiet area of Scotland which is very close to the sea and completely free from pollution.

(2) .... only having about 350 people, my village is quite busy, especially in summer (3) .... all the tourists come.

(4) .... coming to get the ferry to the islands, they also come here to see the castle by the loch (like a lake).

(5) .... as you can imagine, most people here work for the ferry company or in hotels and souvenir shops.

(6) .... Dunlochry is quite far north, it has a mild climate (7) .... of the Gulf Stream. One of my neighbours even has a palm tree in his garden! The landscape is very mountainous and (8) .... there is very little flat land available for farming. Sheep farming has been carried out here for centuries (9) .... , and is quite profitable.

(10) .... , a large number of the local women make money in the winter from knitting the wool into sweaters.

That's all for now. Write and let me know something about where you live in your next letter.

Best wishes,

Susan

Grammar

some, any, no, every

5 *Some, any, no* and *every* can combine with *thing, body/one* and *where* to form a compound. Complete the sentences below using an appropriate form.

a Have you got .... I can read on the way home?

b Peter left without telling .... where he was going.

c She's really well travelled. She's been ....

d .... told me that the trains were on strike.

e Surely we can do .... to make our streets safer.

f Believe me, he really does live five kilometres from ....

g Ministers usually have .... to say when they are asked what they are doing to help the environment.

h .... I know is a non-smoker, so I don't need any ashtrays.

i The policeman told us that .... we said would be taken down and could be used in evidence against us.

G ⇢ STUDENT'S BOOK **page 203**

TOO MANY PEOPLE? 33

16 Eat to live

Reading

1 You are going to read about five people who are vegetarian. For questions 1–14, choose from the people (A–E). The people may be chosen more than once. When more than one answer is required, these may be given in any order.

Which person or people

was influenced by someone?	1	
have joined an organisation to find out more?	2	3
has always enjoyed cooking?	4	
are vegetarian for moral reasons?	5	6
had some problems at first?	7	8
took a while to decide to change?	9	
suffers physically after eating meat?	10	
live with people who don't completely agree with them?	11	12
never enjoyed eating meat?	13	14

If you think that very few people are vegetarian, then you are out of date. Seven per cent of the UK population – that's more than four million people – are now vegetarian. Around 12–14 per cent of teenagers are also thought to be vegetarian, and more are becoming so every day. So what's brought about this change?

A HELEN

Helen has been a vegetarian for twelve and a half years. She says, 'I've never really liked meat, and throughout my teens ate less and less of it. Then, I went abroad on holiday one year and when I came back I decided to give up meat for good. I stopped overnight. I'm more interested in food and cooking now than I used to be. My husband and I love food and we spend hours experimenting with different recipes – there's so much you can do with vegetarian food. Our favourite foods are mainly Italian and Indian. We probably eat too much fat in our diet and are aware that we need to cut down. We're not that keen on brown rice and lentils. I also hate things that try to imitate meat. I study labels carefully but we don't worry too much when we eat out. My husband isn't a vegetarian and this is his one chance to eat meat.'

B BECKY

Becky has been a vegetarian for six months. 'It was my New Year's Resolution,' she says. 'It's been a real eye-opener. I didn't realise that a lot of things I eat – like sauces – have meat products in them. I became a member of the Vegetarian Society, which sent me lots of really helpful information. It's made me realise how much goes into our food and how little we consumers know. I eat lots of pasta and lentils because they are so cheap and easy to prepare. At first I put on a lot of weight because of all the cheese I was eating. Now I'm much better at experimenting with food and I'm enjoying cooking new things. I'm now trying to convince the other people in my flat to become vegetarian too.'

C KATIE

Having a vegetarian boyfriend at school led Katie to think about giving up meat. Then, when she was in her twenties, a TV programme about meat gave her the final push. 'I gave it up there and then,' she says. 'I did worry about my kids eating only vegetarian food, but my doctor says it's fine. As a family, we eat lots of fresh food, pasta and lentils, and try to eat organic food – although it's not always easy. I do use convenience food as I work full-time. We don't often eat puddings and usually have fresh fruit after a meal. The children have the worst time because their friends tell them it's unhealthy to be vegetarian. However, the children know about how badly animals are treated and because of that they are keen to stay vegetarian.'

D JANE

'I love vegetarian food and eat it at least four days a week, sometimes more,' says Jane. 'I prefer the taste, textures and flavours – there are so many interesting ingredients to choose from. I've never been a great meat eater, even as a child, but I haven't been persuaded to cut out meat entirely, as I love dishes like chicken curry and salmon. I've been a keen cook for years. I find chicken and fish easier to cook than vegetarian meals because vegetarianism is new to me. I'm getting better at cooking vegetarian meals though. Being vegetarian has made me more aware of my health. When I do eat meat, I feel sleepy and slow.'

E CHRIS

Chris has strong principles, which is why he became a vegetarian. 'I've always been concerned about the way humans treat animals and I've been vegetarian since I was twelve,' he says. 'However, in the end, vegetarianism just wasn't enough. I felt guilty that I was only making a half-hearted effort, so two years ago, I became a vegan. Now I don't eat any animal produce at all – no milk, eggs, and even honey. It sounds impossible to some people, but it's amazing how easily you adapt. There are alternatives to virtually everything these days. It doesn't even have to cost more. I've found a specialist shop in my town and I've become a member of the Vegan Society, which has given me lots of advice.'

Vocabulary

2 The introduction to the article talks about being *out of date*. Complete the sentences below using one of these *out of* expressions.

> out of breath   out of reach   out of danger
> out of sight   out of order   out of stock
> out of practice   out of work   out of the question

a It's such a long time since I made a cake that I'm ....

b Joanna was taken to hospital after swallowing the fishbone, but now she's ....

c I went to buy a new saucepan, only to be told it was ....

d The kids asked me if they could do the cooking at the weekend and I told them it was ....

e I've been looking through the newspaper ads every day as I've been .... for the last three months.

f I wonder why supermarkets always put the things I want on the top shelf ....

g He's put on so much weight recently, it's no wonder he's .... when he runs.

h I prefer restaurants that prepare food .... I just want to see the finished version!

i When I tried unsuccessfully to get some coffee from the machine I realised it was ....

Grammar

3 Fill the gaps in the following sentences with *a, an, the* or – (when no article is needed).

a We went out for .... meal at .... restaurant where we first met.

b Why are .... potatoes so popular with .... British?

c We flew across .... Atlantic Ocean by .... Concorde to .... United States.

d .... apple .... day keeps .... doctor away, or so they say.

e I worked as .... waitress in .... summer before I went to .... university.

f I think .... coffee is .... best drink in .... world.

g Susan was invited to .... dinner party at .... Jane's last week.

h When we go abroad we always bring back some of .... food and .... drink that we enjoyed.

G ⇢ STUDENT'S BOOK **page 204**

4 The article below is about the American-Chinese chef Ken Hom. For questions 1–10 think of the word which best fits each gap. Use only one word in each gap. There is an example at the beginning (0).

Ken Hom

I started cooking in my uncle's Chinese restaurant (0) ...*at*... the age of 11. At first, I just washed the dishes, then chopped and sliced the vegetables. But as soon (1) .... the chefs went out of the kitchen I'd try to copy the dishes I'd seen (2) .... cook. The first dish I attempted to make was fried rice. It's (3) .... difficult to mess up that anyone can cook it.

By the (4) .... I was 15 I was fed (5) .... working 12-hour days in the restaurant. So, I (6) .... up my mind to go to university to study History of Art and only started cooking again when I needed some extra money.

I think Americans eat too (7) .... fat. Chinese food is much healthier. My mission (8) .... always been to encourage people to eat (9) .... fat and meat and more vegetables. Kids say they don't eat vegetables, but they usually haven't had them stir fried. Cooked (10) .... this they are delicious, healthy and fun.

EAT TO LIVE   35

17 Collectors and creators

Vocabulary

1 Read this short article about unusual hobbies. Then use the word given in capitals at the end of some of the lines to form a word that fits in the gap in the same line. There is an example at the beginning (0).

Playing tiddlywinks

Haggis hurling

An inn sign

STRANGE PURSUITS

Go through the Directory of British Associations and you'll find about 7,000 groups that are considered large enough to be of national (0) *importance* . **IMPORTANT**

However, with the (1) .... of every local gardening club, film society and special interest group, the number swells to around 150,000! **INCLUDE**

Most of these clubs provide a meeting place for like-minded people. Societies and associations cater for every (2) .... interest, from cheese appreciation to the history of wallpaper. **IMAGINE**

With such an (3) .... choice available, there must quite literally be something for everyone. Let's kick off with the Haggis* Hurling Association, which supervises what has become a *Guinness Book of Records* event (current record for a 680 gram haggis: 55 metres) and organises (4) .... to raise money for good causes. Then there's tiddlywinks. This game, it must be said, has never been the most popular or the most (5) .... , but it has nevertheless had an official association since 1958. Most people start playing tiddlywinks 'for a joke', but then they get hooked, perhaps because most of the post-match (6) .... is done at the pub. **END** **COMPETE** **GLAMOUR** **ANALYSE**

If tiddlywinks strikes you as too (7) .... , the leisurely study of pub signs might be more your cup of tea. The Inn Sign Society has 400 members who spend their time travelling the country in search of (8) .... pub signs. Their founder used to have a (9) .... of 300 actual signs, as well as 20,000 photos of pub signs, going back to the 1930s. **ENERGY** **USUAL** **COLLECT**

To get the addresses of these clubs and others, why not visit your local library? (10) .... , try searching the Internet using Google. You're bound to find something appealing that you've never even thought of! **ALTERNATE**

* A haggis is like a large, round sausage and is eaten in Scotland.

UNIT 17

2 Find words and phrases in the article in 1 that mean the same as a–f.

a grows
b provide
c start
d charities
e become addicted
f certain

3 The article refers to *like-minded* people, meaning people with similar views, and also uses the adverb *likewise*, to introduce a similar idea. How many uses of *like* do you recognise below? They have all appeared in previous units. Complete the sentences using each one once.

| likeness | unlikely | likeable | liking | like |

a Goat-driving seems a very .... hobby to me, but there's an official club listed here!
b Dressing up in old clothes and fighting battles isn't to my ....
c My nephew goes beach-combing for shells, unusual pebbles, and things .... that.
d Once the full make-up has been put on, he shows an amazing .... to Captain Kirk.
e Gerry is a very .... 75-year-old, who enjoys nothing more than dancing to old rock music.

Writing

4 Write a paragraph on haggis hurling, using the rules below. Try to use relative clauses to make your sentences longer, for example:

The Haggis Hurling Association, <u>which was founded in 1977 by Robin Dunseath</u>, challenges people to throw a haggis of a certain weight as far as they can.

Rules
The haggis …
- must be prepared according to the traditional recipe
- should be cooled at the time of hurling
- will be inspected for illegal firming agents such as cement
- must not break or split on landing (this results in disqualification)
- should weigh 500 grams (junior and middle weight events) or up to 1 kg (heavyweight event)
- should have a maximum diameter of 18 cm and length of 22 cm (junior and middle weight events).

Grammar

5 For questions 1–12, read the text below and think of the word which best fits each gap. Use only **one** word in each gap. There is an example at the beginning (0).

Elisabeth Daborn, 27, (0) ......who...... works for a local newspaper, and software engineer Kevin Cowley, 34, spend most of their weekends fighting. However, (1) .... is nothing personal! They both belong (2) .... Regia Angolorum, one of Britain's three main Viking societies. Elisabeth explains their shared passion. 'Kevin used to (3) .... keen on LARPing – Live Action Role Play – but after (4) .... while, he decided he wanted something more authentic. So he joined Regia, (5) .... specialism is the period 950 to 1066. The society organises battles (6) .... over the country and the terms of our insurance mean that we have to attend regular battle practice sessions. Because there's (7) .... proof that Viking women fought, I dress up (8) .... a man. We get offered quite a (9) .... of film work. Recently, Regia's been in a TV series and on a rock video, (10) .... we had to row our longship and headbang at the same time. The longship, (11) .... was built for the film *Erik the Viking*, is safe to use on rivers, (12) .... I wouldn't like to go out to sea on it!'

COLLECTORS AND CREATORS 37

18 What's in a book?

Reading

1 You are going to read a magazine article about the writer Daphne du Maurier. Seven sentences have been removed from the article. Choose from the sentences A–H the one which fits each gap (1–7). There is one extra sentence which you do not need to use.

Daphne du Maurier

Often seen only as a writer of popular romances, Daphne du Maurier's work is much more complex than that. To mark the centenary of her birth this month, Patrick McGrath relishes the dark side of her short stories …

Daphne du Maurier was born into a famous London theatrical family, but lived in Cornwall for most of her life, in a large romantic house near the sea called Menabilly. **1** There can be no doubt that Menabilly and its surroundings inspired several of her novels and short stories.

Du Maurier enjoyed early success as a writer and continued to have a wide readership throughout her career, with bestsellers such as *Jamaica Inn*, *The House on the Strand* and, of course, *Rebecca*. **2** He also adapted her spine-chilling short story *The Birds*, choosing to set it in northern California rather than in its originally wild Cornish location. Apparently, Daphne du Maurier hated this adaptation.

Before writing her collection of short stories *The Apple Tree*, to which *The Birds* belonged, du Maurier had been known for her romantic fiction. She had made her mark in particular with historical novels such as *Frenchman's Creek* and *Jamaica Inn*. However, *The Birds* was not inspired by the past. **3** Arguably, it was the starting point for an entire genre devoted to narratives about natural disaster.

The Apple Tree collection was published in 1952. **4** It is about a man in an unhappy marriage, whose wife Midge suddenly dies. Bizarrely, he starts to hate a particular apple tree in his garden, as he sees in it his dead wife's most irritating characteristics. He decides to get rid of it once and for all. Eventually the tree destroys him, and we understand that it is through his own bad feelings towards Midge that he has brought this end upon himself.

Nature in du Maurier's stories rarely has a favourable effect on humans, other than in the coming-of-age story called *The Pool*. This beautiful tale takes place in the middle of summer in the English countryside. By a woodland pool, a girl finds a 'secret world' – a strange underwater place with fantastic beings. **5** This is nature as it is experienced by a child: magical, enchanting, and unreal. With the end of childhood, her secret world is out of reach for ever.

In a powerful story called *The Chamois*, we follow a husband and wife as they go up a mountain in northern Greece. The tensions in the marriage are quickly established, as is the man's obsession with hunting that elusive animal, the chamois. Having reached the top of a mountain pass, the couple are taken into the high regions by a shepherd. What follows in the story reveals the truth of each character's nature, in a manner not unlike that of the Ernest Hemingway hunting story *The Short Happy Life of Francis Macomber*. **6** It is the actions of the woman that are especially surprising in du Maurier's tale, just as they are in the Hemingway one.

Daphne du Maurier wrote exciting plots, and was highly skilled at creating suspense. **7** Indeed, in her lifetime she published more than three dozen works of fiction, history and biography. A new edition of *Don't Look Now and Other Stories* will be published by the Folio Society in the autumn.

A While the title story lacks the tension of *The Birds*, there are similarities in its treatment of nature.

B Not only this, she was also a writer of fearless originality, whose imagination served her well over the years.

C What she in fact discovers is the power of her own imagination.

D Alfred Hitchcock turned this wonderful tale into a memorable film of the same name.

E The bandages are removed and, to the woman's astonishment and horror, everyone she sees has the head of an animal.

F Although she never owned it, she adored living there and it was where she raised her family.

G The climax of this story similarly involves a guide, a beast and a gun.

H It seemed instead to look ahead to major environmental catastrophe in the near future.

Vocabulary

2 Find 14 more words to do with books and writing in this wordsearch. Words can be horizontal or vertical.

F	T	H	R	I	L	L	E	R	A	N	E
I	L	L	U	S	T	R	A	T	I	O	N
C	T	P	A	O	T	C	L	E	O	V	N
T	R	U	C	X	C	H	A	P	T	E	R
I	H	B	T	L	R	A	N	H	I	L	P
O	N	L	I	C	K	R	Y	T	U	I	L
N	B	I	O	G	R	A	P	H	Y	S	O
W	E	S	N	C	S	C	E	N	E	T	T
Y	O	H	R	A	O	T	T	F	T	N	L
K	E	E	H	L	M	E	V	E	N	T	A
X	O	R	A	M	I	R	E	V	I	E	W
W	E	S	T	O	R	Y	O	P	L	A	Y

3 Name the phrasal verbs with *come* and *go* that fit definitions a–h.

a face (a difficulty)
....

b sink or fail
....

c endure
....

d ebb or recede
....

e fall
....

f be deprived of
....

g chase
....

h bloom
....

Grammar

so, such, too, very, enough

4 Correct the following sentences if necessary.

a I have never read a such long book as this one.
b The story was very complicated that I gave up.
c Hardback books are too much expensive.
d Enough books weren't ordered.
e I was too sad to reach the end of that novel.
f It was a such exciting plot.
g The print in this paperback isn't enough big.
h Characters as these are quite unusual.

5 Complete the text by putting *so, such, too, very* or *enough* in gaps 1–15.

The Old Man and the Sea is (1) .... easy to read and it isn't (2) .... long a book, either. You may find the story (3) .... compelling to put down. On the (4) .... first page, you learn that the old man has gone 84 days without catching (5) .... much as a single fish.

On that opening page, almost everything about him is described as old – characteristics (6) .... as the wrinkles on his neck and the many scars on his hands. Interestingly (7) ...., however, you are also told that his eyes are not old; they are 'cheerful' and 'undefeated'. This makes you feel (8) .... enormous sympathy for the old man. You want him to bring home another fish (9) .... soon, before he becomes (10) .... old to go out to sea. I think the reason why the book is (11) .... popular is that it tells a (12) .... simple story that is timeless (13) .... to appeal to people of all ages and backgrounds. It has (14) .... an unusual style, (15) .... , which contributes to its success.

G ···▸ STUDENT'S BOOK **page 205**

WHAT'S IN A BOOK? **39**

19 An apple a day ...

Reading

1 You are going to read a newspaper article about how dancing can be good for your health. For questions 1–7, choose the answer (A, B, C or D) which you think fits best according to the text.

Flo Marsden, aged 71, is learning how to belly dance thanks to a local dance scheme in the UK. Janet Booth reports.

Dance is increasingly being introduced to anyone who is interested for both health and recreational reasons. The National Lottery is funding courses and training, as are local authorities and regional arts associations. In addition, family doctors are prescribing dance to patients, and young footballers are learning about rhythm and balance through hip-hop lessons. There is barely a hall in the country that does not shudder with the sound of stamping feet every week.

The Yorkshire Dance Centre runs Flo's classes. Simon Dove, the dance centre's organiser and promoter, says that attendance has doubled in the last three years. He attributes this to more choice and easier access. And what a choice there is! There are 35 different lessons every week – everything from Arabic dancing to Egyptian, American tap, Asian and South African Township dance. 'Aerobics and fitness regimes can be an introspective and solitary way of keeping fit,' Simon explains. 'People like coming here because it helps you stay fit and engages your mind, forcing you to interact with others.'

Steve Johnson, 28, is one of the company's teachers. He goes into schools and introduces kids to jazz, street dance and hip hop. He thinks that for the less academic, it gives them something to focus on. 'Several school teachers have reported back to me that normally difficult and disruptive children have become more manageable because of the lessons. I think it is because they have found something at school that they excel at, making them more confident. The lessons also make them more aware of their bodies and how they work.'

For Flo, who already keeps fit by doing aerobics, her weekly dance lessons play a more social role in her life. 'It's the togetherness of dancing that is the best. A Keep Fit class doesn't get you so involved with others. When I go out shopping I see people from the lessons and say hello. It makes you feel you are part of a community.' 37

Dance is one of the five activities the Health Education Authority is promoting in its current Active for Life campaign, and this summer saw one of the first health and dance conferences in the UK. John Dunbar, one of the speakers, says that on a fitness level, dance can be just as effective as going on a running programme: 'There were tests done in the US where two previously sedentary 30-year-olds were put on fitness programmes, one using dance, the other running, and the results were the same. People are far more likely to keep dancing up rather than a running programme, so in that way it can be more suitable.'

So, if you're lucky enough to have dance classes near where you live, my advice to you would be to have a go!

1 The dance classes are being paid for by
 A the participants themselves.
 B a variety of public bodies.
 C family health centres.
 D local sports centres.

2 What does Simon say about the dance classes in the second paragraph?
 A Some are more popular than others.
 B They are the quickest way to make friends.
 C They are a very sociable way to exercise.
 D There is no limit to the number you can take.

3 Steve Johnson believes that dance
 A is suitable for the less active type of child.
 B has grown in popularity in less academic schools.
 C can be taught by ordinary school teachers.
 D helps children who have low self-esteem.

4 Flo enjoys going to dance classes because
 A they make her feel more relaxed than other classes.
 B they provide her with a sense of belonging.
 C they allow her to meet people from outside the area.
 D they have enabled her to get over her shyness.

5 What does 'It' refer to in line 37?
 A dancing
 B a community
 C keeping fit
 D the social role

6 According to John Dunbar, dancing
 A is much better for you than running.
 B needs to be done regularly to be effective.
 C has most effect on the health of older people.
 D motivates people more than running.

Vocabulary

2 Find the ten 'health' words in this wordsearch. Some words are parts of the body and others are connected with doctors and hospitals. Words can be horizontal, vertical or diagonal. They may run forwards and backwards.

B	A	N	D	A	G	E	B	H	L
G	N	D	H	W	A	L	L	C	Q
U	K	I	G	I	T	B	K	A	S
F	L	U	U	A	B	O	R	M	T
Y	E	R	O	Y	N	W	T	O	K
M	H	R	C	U	E	N	D	T	N
S	H	A	O	L	X	I	F	S	E
T	E	H	E	A	D	A	C	H	E
Q	R	Y	M	L	D	P	V	N	O
I	N	J	E	C	T	I	O	N	P

Grammar

3 Complete the second sentence so that it has a similar meaning to the first sentence, using the word given. **Do not change the word given.** You must use between two and five words, including the word given.

1. You really should try to stop smoking.
   high
   It's .... smoking.

2. He advised me to do some weight training.
   were
   'If ....
   do some weight training,' he said.

3. 'Why don't we go for a walk next weekend?' Anne said.
   suggested
   Anne ....
   for a walk the following weekend.

4. What do you think I should do?
   advise
   What .... do?

5. Your teeth need checking regularly.
   have
   You ought ....
   regularly.

6. I would strongly advise you to get your blood pressure checked.
   time
   It's ....
   blood pressure checked.

7. Before you go abroad, you should have an injection.
   had
   Before you go abroad, ...
   .... an injection.

8. It's not a good idea to sit in the sun for too long.
   better
   You ....
   in the sun for too long.

G ⋯⋰ STUDENT'S BOOK **page 205**

Writing

4 You are living in London. You have received a letter from your English-speaking friend, Sally, who is coming to stay with you while she looks for a flat of her own. Read Sally's letter and the advertisement for the fitness centre, together with the notes you have made. Then write a letter to Sally, using all your notes. Write your answer in 120–150 words in an appropriate style. Do not write any postal addresses.

> I want to continue keeping fit while I'm staying with you. Can you find out about your local fitness centre for me? I prefer going in the early morning before work, if that's possible? Also do I have to do a special introductory course to get to know the equipment? Are there any discounts for people under 25 or for regular users? Maybe you'd like to join and come with me in the mornings?

give her details

prefer dance at weekends

Bodytone Fitness Centre

We're open seven days a week from 6.30am to 10.30pm.
Buy a weekly or monthly ticket and come as many times as you please. There are discounts for the under 18s and the over 60s.
A weekly ticket is £25 or monthly £65.
Dance classes available at weekends – salsa, line dancing and jazz dance.
Telephone to book your introductory session with our fully trained staff. NB This is compulsory for all users of the centre.

AN APPLE A DAY ... 41

20 No place to hide

Vocabulary

1 Complete the sentences below.

 a The opposite of guilty is _____ .
 b Murderers are usually _____ to life imprisonment.
 c _____ are people who see a crime being committed.
 d In a court there is usually a ____ of twelve men or women.
 e The accused person is called the _____ .
 f The police have to produce _____ that you have committed a crime.
 g For speeding you will usually be given a ____ .

2 For questions 1–10, read the text below. Use the word given in capitals to form a word that fits in the gap.

White-collar Crime

White-collar crime is defined as (1) .... (LEGAL) acts committed by middle or upper-class people while at work. The term gained (2) .... (POPULAR) in 1940 when it was first used by the American criminologist Edwin H. Sutherland. Sutherland argued that there were important sociological (3) .... (DIFFERENT) between conventional crimes such as (4) .... (BURGLAR) and murder, and white-collar crimes such as fraud and income tax (5) .... (EVADE). In general, the latter are committed by persons of (6) .... (RELATIVE) high social status and are treated more leniently than are more (7) .... (CONVENTION) crimes. White-collar crime has become an (8) .... (INCREASE) problem. The authorities are now dealing with such crimes more severely because of a growing feeling that an effort must be made to establish (9) .... (EQUAL) before the law for all citizens – (10) .... (REGARD) of money, power or social status.

Idioms

3 The idiom 'to be caught red-handed' means to be discovered doing something wrong or illegal. Match the sentences in A, which use other colour idioms, with the sentences in B, which explain their meaning.

A
1 The invitation to the wedding arrived out of the blue.
2 He went green when he saw the Ferrari that his neighbour had bought.
3 Even though I try to budget I'm perpetually in the red.
4 My uncle has been the black sheep of the family ever since he went to prison for fraud.
5 Anna told her friend a white lie so she could get out of going to her party.
6 Stephen came home in a really black mood after being told he wasn't going to get a pay rise this year.

B
a feeling very depressed
b overdrawn at the bank
c being slightly dishonest
d to be envious
e as a surprise
f someone who has brought disgrace to the family

Grammar

4 For questions 1–12, read the text below and think of the word which best fits each gap. Use only one word in each gap. There is an example at the beginning (0).

A bad experience

Thank you (0) ......**for**...... the photos you sent me of our holiday together. It was great to remember (1) .... a good time we had, especially as I've not had a very happy time (2) .... I got back. (3) .... you know, I'm a member of the city choir and we meet every Wednesday to practise. Well, two weeks (4) .... I went to the meeting as usual. However, on (5) .... way to the bus stop a young woman stopped me and asked me for directions (6) .... a local park. I thought it was rather strange as it was already dark and the park (7) .... definitely be closed. Anyway, as I was telling (8) .... she pushed me over and ran off with my handbag. I was (9) .... shocked I didn't know what to do. A few minutes later, although it felt (10) .... a few hours, someone came along the street and saw me (11) .... the ground. They were very helpful and took me to the local police station. I told the police what had happened but they don't think there's (12) .... chance of my getting my bag back, unfortunately.

Gerund or infinitive

5 Correct the following sentences where necessary.

a He suggested to buy a detective novel.
b I look forward to hear the results of the case.
c I enjoy watching American cop programmes.
d The burglar alarm needs to be seeing to.
e Let me giving you a description of the mugger.
f The prisoners were made to sew mail bags.
g I can't afford taking a taxi all the time just to avoid the Underground.
h The tourist was accustomed to drive his car faster in his country.
i You are not allowed dropping litter on the street.
j I'd like reporting a burglary.
k She's too small to drive a car.

G STUDENT'S BOOK **page 206**

Thank you so much for inviting me
perhaps we will meet again soon
looking forward to your talk on 5th November
marvellous that you can tell
Me and my family would love to come
So much from a person's handwriting
we spent the day at their house
sorry I haven't written for so long

Writing

6 Read through this article on 'graphology', and correct any spelling errors you find. There are twelve errors.

Graphology is the study and analysis of handwriting in order to asess the writer's personality. In crime detection, graphology is used to determine the authenticity of a signature or docuement, such as a will or manuscript, witout concern for the writer's personality. Graphologists need at least a full-page ink specimen, writen spontaneously under normal phisical conditions, by a person able to write with ease. Before the analysis, the graphologist must know the writer's age, sex, and nationality, none of wich is revealed by the writing itself. Handwriting conssists of measureable elements, such as slant and size, and of descriptive elements, such as letter form and tendencies to the right and left. However, allthough the results of handwriting analysis sometimes correspond impresively with experimental evidence, graphology has still not been fully acepted as a legitimate branch of phsychology.

21 To have and have not

Reading

1 Read this extract from a book, where an unusual shop is described.
What do you think the writer does for a living and why is he in America?

It had been boring hanging about the hotel all afternoon. The road crew were playing a game with dollar notes, folding them into small planes to see whose would fly the furthest. Having nothing better to do, I joined in and won five, and then took the opportunity to escape with my profit. Despite the evil-looking clouds, I had to get out for a while.

I headed for a shop on the other side of the street. Unlike the others, it didn't have a sign shouting its name and business, and instead of the usual impersonal modern lighting, there was an appealing glow inside. Strangely, nothing was displayed in the window. Not put off by this, I went inside.

It took my breath away. I didn't know where to look, where to start. On one wall there hung three hand-stitched American quilts that were in such wonderful condition they might have been newly-made. I came across tin toys and antique furniture, and on the wall in front of me, a 1957 Stratocaster guitar, also in excellent condition. A card pushed between the strings said $50. I ran my hand along a long shelf of records, reading their titles. And there was more ...

'Can I help you?' She startled me. I hadn't even seen the woman behind the counter come in. The way she looked at me, so directly and with such power. It was a look of such intensity that for a moment I felt as if I were wrapped in some kind of magnetic or electrical field. I found it hard to take and almost turned away. But though it was uncomfortable, I was fascinated by the experience of her looking straight into me, and by the feeling that I was neither a stranger, nor strange, to her.

Besides amusement her expression showed sympathy. It was impossible to tell her age within twenty years; she reminded me faintly of my grandmother because, although her eyes were friendly, I could see that she was not a woman to fall out with. I spoke at last. 'I was just looking really,' I said, though secretly wondering how much of the stuff I could cram into the bus.

The woman turned away and went at once towards a back room, indicating that I should follow her. But it in no way lived up to the first room. The light made me feel peculiar, too. It came from an oil lamp that was hung from the centre of the ceiling and created huge shadows over everything. There were no rare electric guitars, no old necklaces, no hand-painted boxes with delicate flowers. It was also obvious that it must have taken years, decades, to collect so much rubbish, so many old documents and papers.

I noticed some old books, whose gold lettering had faded, making their titles impossible to read. 'They look interesting,' I said, with some hesitation. 'To be able to understand that kind of writing you must first have had a similar experience,' she said clearly. She noted the confused look on my face, but didn't add anything.

She reached up for a small book which she handed to me. 'This is the best book I can give you at the moment,' she laughed. 'If you use it.' I opened the book to find it full, or rather empty, with blank white pages, but paid her the few dollars she asked for it, becoming embarrassed when I realised the notes were still folded into little paper planes. I put the book in my pocket, thanked her and left.

Taken from 'The Big Wheel' by Bruce Thomas, formerly bass guitarist with Elvis Costello and the Attractions

44 UNIT 21

2 Now read the extract again. For questions 1–6, choose the answer **A, B, C or D** which you think fits best according to the text.

1 Why did the writer want to leave the hotel?
   A to enjoy the good weather
   B to have a change of scene
   C to spend all his winnings
   D to get away from the crew

2 What encouraged the writer to enter the shop?
   A the lack of a sign or name
   B the fact that it was nearby
   C the empty window display
   D the light coming from inside

3 The writer found the stock in the front of the shop
   A of top quality.
   B of good value.
   C difficult to get at.
   D badly displayed.

4 What was unusual about the way the woman looked at him?
   A It made him feel self-conscious.
   B She was happy to stare at him.
   C She seemed to know who he was.
   D It made him want to look away.

5 The writer disliked the back room because
   A there was hardly anything in it.
   B she had ordered him to go there.
   C he saw nothing he really liked.
   D it was too dark to look around.

6 Why did the woman refuse to show him the old books?
   A They had pages which were too faint to read.
   B She decided they wouldn't mean anything to him.
   C She understood that he wasn't interested in them.
   D They were only for display in the shop.

3 Find five phrasal verbs in the text with the meanings below (the paragraph where each occurs is given in brackets).

   a waiting idly (1) ....
   b discouraged (2) ....
   c found (3) ....
   d disagree with (5) ....
   e matched (6) ....

Grammar
Conjunctions

4 Match the two sentence halves, joining them with a suitable conjunction from the list below. Sometimes more than one conjunction can be used.

> because   despite   even though   in case
> in spite of   so   whereas   while

a Accounts in credit are normally free
b It's worth phoning the shop first
c I hate going to the January sales
d The market stalls sell a range of vegetables
e I really enjoy browsing at a bookshop
f Refusing to give a refund is against the law
g City councils no longer encourage out-of-town shopping sites
h I've had this computer less than a year but there's a new model available

1 they're not always as fresh as they could be.
2 the shops are all so crowded.
3 five years ago they were actively promoting them.
4 what some shops claim.
5 banks charge a lot for an overdraft.
6 mine is already out of date.
7 making an order by computer doesn't have any appeal.
8 the goods you require are out of stock.

Vocabulary

5 Match each definition to a word from the box.

> account   balance   branches   capital
> cashpoint   debit   interest   overdraft
> statement   withdraw

a The amount you have at your bank.
b If you have one of these, you are 'in the red'.
c Money earned on an investment.
d You do this when you take out money.
e A sum of money that has been invested.
f A machine where you can get money.
g You have your money in this at a bank.
h This is sent to you monthly or quarterly.
i A bank has many of these in a city.
j The bank does this when they take money from your account.

TO HAVE AND HAVE NOT   45

22 A little night music

Vocabulary

1 For questions 1–12, read the text below and decide which answer (A, B, C or D) best fits each gap. There is an example at the beginning (0).

Example:
0   A crammed   B filled   C pressed   D placed
Answer: A

The sonic tool that has shaped pop music

Imagine having a full orchestra (0) ..... into your house. For a start, with so many people, it would get very stuffy indeed. The patience of the (1) ..... would soon wear thin. Also, you would need earplugs for the percussion, and the brass (2) ..... would probably drink everything in your fridge. An acceptable alternative is (3) ..... by the sampler, a piece of equipment that records, edits and mixes a (4) ..... variety of sounds electronically – the musical equivalent of a word processor.

The sampler can alter the length of sounds – for example, it can (5) ..... down the human voice to (6) ..... something very unusual. Another feature is that the recorded sound can be (7) ..... back at any pitch – the woof of a small dog can be (8) ..... into a Bark prelude and fugue! Joking (9) ..... , the first digitally-sampled sounds did in fact belong to a dog.

1980s 'synth-pop' (10) ..... extensive use of the sampler. It was customary to include orchestral 'stabs': a single, short (11) ..... from an entire symphony orchestra inside a tin box. Then hip-hop music (12) ..... and people started using the sampler for rhythm, stealing four bars of drumming off an old record to provide the backbeat for a whole song. It could be said that the sampler is every instrument and none, but it certainly gives endless possibilities to musicians everywhere.

1	A controller	B governor	C driver	D conductor
2	A team	B section	C group	D band
3	A handled	B offered	C shown	D suggested
4	A wide	B deep	C high	D broad
5	A cut	B hold	C slow	D keep
6	A discover	B bring	C create	D lead
7	A played	B gone	C taken	D run
8	A got	B turned	C exchanged	D set
9	A beside	B alone	C aside	D only
10	A did	B put	C drew	D made
11	A note	B key	C sign	D remark
12	A caused	B became	C happened	D produced

2 Find the odd word out in each of the sets a–h, giving reasons for your answers.

a flute   harp   performance   oboe
b violinist   pianist   vocalist   conductor
c gig   recital   concert   festival
d piece   key   sonata   symphony
e improvise   compose   perform   play
f duo   soloist   quartet   orchestra
g venue   hall   room   stage
h wind   strings   bass   percussion

Writing

3 Read the following article about live concerts. Then put clauses A–G into the correct gaps (1–6) in the article. There is one extra clause, which you do not need to use.

Seeing live music

There's something very special about going to a live concert. Although CDs are wonderful, allowing you to listen to your favourite band in the comfort of your own home, they cannot create the true atmosphere of a live performance. **(1)** ..... , or sent off for them months before, you get the same feeling of excitement when you finally make it into the concert venue. **(2)** ..... , you eventually see the road crew leave the stage. **(3)** ..... , with everyone around you yelling and screaming, as the musicians come on stage? **(4)** ..... , you soon get carried away by the rhythm and power of the music. **(5)** ..... , the audience around you rocks and sways to the beat of each song. **(6)** ..... , you stomp your feet and shout for more, and are rewarded at last by the sight of the band running back on stage for that final encore. Give me live music every time!

A How can you keep still after that
B Even if it is not your favourite band
C Whether you have queued up for tickets
D And when it seems to be over
E Standing with thousands of other fans
F Like waves in a heavy sea
G This is doubly true then

23 Unexpected events

Vocabulary

1 Find the fourteen 'weather' words in this wordsearch. Words can be horizontal, vertical or diagonal. They may run forwards and backwards.

Y	L	I	G	H	T	N	I	N	G	N	U
Q	B	D	A	M	P	V	C	A	A	N	P
F	Z	C	V	H	A	I	L	E	L	E	R
L	H	P	O	S	S	W	Q	U	E	F	I
O	X	V	M	R	O	T	S	M	G	L	O
O	Z	Y	J	N	K	O	U	C	L	A	P
D	I	E	S	L	R	E	W	O	H	S	P
S	E	A	Q	I	R	E	D	N	U	H	T
W	G	T	U	F	O	R	E	C	A	S	T
O	I	R	A	I	N	D	R	O	P	R	B
R	S	S	Q	W	P	M	N	E	U	T	Y
H	U	R	R	I	C	A	N	E	E	R	T

Reading

2 Before you read the text, think about the following questions and decide whether they are true or false.

   a You are safer in your house than in your car, if lightning strikes.
   b There is a fair chance you will be struck by lightning.
   c Many forest fires are started by lightning.
   d You must keep away from trees if there is a chance of lightning striking.
   e If you are caught in a storm, you should crouch down as low as possible on the ground.

3 Now skim the text quickly to see if you can find the answers to the questions above.

4 For questions 1–15, choose from the sections (A–G). The sections may be chosen more than once.

Which section(s)

talks about a gadget?	1		
refers to a person who has changed the way she/he does something?	2		
mentions a person who only appeared unharmed on the outside?	3		
mention victims being in an open space?	4	5	
mentions a myth?	6		
states that someone was brought back to life?	7		
mentions a lucky escape?	8		
refer to unexpected effects of lightning?	9	10	11
blames lightning for a natural disaster?	12		
offer advice?	13	14	
mentions a person who was given wrong information?	15		

48 UNIT 23

Lightning strikes!

A Three years ago a bolt of lightning all but destroyed Lyn Miller's house in Aberdeen – with her two children inside. 'There was a huge rainstorm,' she says, recalling the terrifying experience. 'My brother and I were outside desperately working to stop floodwater from coming in the house. Suddenly I was thrown to the ground by an enormous bang. When I picked myself up, the roof and the entire upper storey of the house had been demolished. The door was blocked by rubble, but we forced our way in and found the children, thankfully unharmed. Later I was told to be struck by lightning is a chance in a million.' In fact, it's calculated at one chance in 600,000. Even so, Dr Mark Keys of AER Technology, an organisation that monitors the effects of lightning, thinks you should be sensible. 'I wouldn't go out in a storm – but then I'm quite a careful person.' He advises anyone who is unlucky enough to be caught in a storm to get down on the ground and curl up into a ball, making yourself as small as possible.

B Lightning is one of nature's most awesome displays of sheer power. No wonder the ancient Greeks thought it was Zeus, father of the gods, throwing thunderbolts around in anger. 250 years ago, Benjamin Franklin, the American scientist and statesman, proved that lightning is a form of electricity, but scientists still lack a complete understanding of how it works.

C Occasionally there are warning signs. Positive electrical charges streaming upwards from trees or church spires may glow and make a buzzing noise, and people's hair can stand on end. And if you fear lightning, you'll be glad to know that a company in the USA has manufactured a hand-held lightning detector which can detect it up to 70 kms away, sound a warning tone and monitor the storm's approach.

D Nancy Wilder was playing golf at a club in Surrey when she was hit by a bolt of lightning. Mrs Wilder's heart stopped beating, but she was resuscitated and, after a few days in hospital, where she was treated for burns to her head, hands and feet, she was pronounced fit again. Since that time, she has been a strictly fair weather golfer. In fact, a golf course is one of the most dangerous places to be during a thunderstorm. The best place to be is inside a car!

E The largest number of people to be struck by lightning at one time was in September 1995 when 17 players on a football pitch were hit simultaneously. The most extraordinary aspect of the strike was the fact that 11 of the victims – seven adults and four children – had burn patterns of tiny holes at 3 centimetre intervals on each toe and around the soles of their feet.

F Harold Deal, a retired electrician from South Carolina, USA, was struck by lightning 26 years ago. He was apparently unhurt, but it later emerged that the strike had damaged the part of the brain which controls the sensation of temperature. Since then the freezing South Carolina winters haven't bothered Harold, since he is completely unable to feel the cold.

G Animals are victims of lightning too. Hundreds of cows and sheep are killed every year, largely because they go under trees. In East Anglia in 1918, 504 sheep were killed instantaneously by the same bolt of lightning that hit the ground and travelled through the entire flock. Lightning is also responsible for starting more than 10,000 forest fires each year world-wide.

5 Find words in the text which are the opposite of these words. They are all in the order you read them.

a outside ....
b forgetting ....
c tiny ....
d lower ....
e irresponsible ....
f fortunate ....
g partial ....
h frequently ....
i negative ....
j unhealthy ....
k safest ....
l boiling ....

Grammar

6 Correct the following sentences, if necessary.

a I hope I would see you soon.
b I wish I would go to visit you.
c Mary said she wished she had been able to come to your party last weekend.
d I hope your family are well.
e If only you manage to give up smoking, just think of the money you'd save.
f I'd rather to stay in a hotel than go camping.
g I hope the weather would stay nice for you.
h I wish my sister would come and see me sometime.
i I wish I haven't seen that film about earthquakes – I can't sleep at night now.
j I wish to inform you of my move to a new job.
k Dave wishes he knows more about earthquakes.
l I would rather you don't speak to me in that tone of voice.

G STUDENT'S BOOK **page 207**

UNEXPECTED EVENTS 49

24 Priceless or worthless?

Grammar

1 For questions 1–12, read the text below and think of the word which best fits each gap. Use only one word in each gap. There is an example at the beginning (0).

Your guides to the best possible taste

Have you ever wondered (0) ...*what*... people generally like in a painting?

In 1993, two artists set (1) .... to discover what America's favourite painting looked (2) .... They hired telephone researchers to call 1,001 Americans from all backgrounds and ask them a list of questions. What (3) .... of paintings do you like? Which colours do you prefer? There were 102 questions (4) .... all. Once equipped with (5) .... information, the artists, Vitaly Komar and Alexander Melamid, began to create two paintings – America's Most Wanted, and America's Most Unwanted. Eighty-eight per cent of people questioned wanted (6) .... landscape. Favourite colours were blue and green. On the (7) .... hand, America's Most Unwanted aimed to displease. (8) .... was 'different looking', featured gold, orange, peach and teal, and was far (9) .... modern. However, this was only the start of the artists' scientific guide to taste. Komar and Melamid then went (10) .... to do similar surveys for another nine countries. Disturbingly, the (11) .... of the respondents in these countries wanted landscapes similar (12) .... the one Americans had chosen.

2 The words in these sentences are jumbled. Put them in the correct order and add punctuation. Sometimes there is more than one correct answer.

a theatre I go often there isn't to town one my don't the very in because
b use I phone could your please
c lovely dress bought her a silk yesterday blue I
d keen never Alan on swimming has been
e members few were a of students quite the audience the of
f Italian very I much like food
g quietly watched pulled they down old cinema as crowd the the
h asked money him the if man he give him some could
i does not also bananas Alison only like she keen apples on is
j been horrified life never I so my in have

G ⇢ STUDENT'S BOOK page 207

50 UNIT 24

Vocabulary

Verb collocations

3 Complete these sentences by using the correct form of one of the verbs below.

| taste | do | sit | spend |
| keep | have | break | get |

a My new car .... 25 kms to the litre.
b Some airline food .... funny.
c People always seem to .... a fortune when they go on holiday.
d I .... a conversation at the bus stop when I realised the person I was talking about was right behind me.
e Why can't you children .... still for more than five minutes?
f His speech was so boring it was all I could do to .... awake.
g Is your brother .... better at playing chess?
h My father said he would lend me his car at the weekend, but he .... his promise.

Adverb–adjective collocations

4 In Unit 24 of the Student's Book, the writer of the article said that Beso's paintings *are very highly thought of*. This means people like them very much and believe that he is a real artist.

Which of the adverbs in A collocate with the adjectives in B?

A
| highly | deeply |
| perfectly | seriously |

B
ill	serious	acclaimed	happy
disappointed	reasonable		
amusing	ashamed		

5 Complete these sentences using the correct collocation from exercise 4.

a John was .... when he failed to win the motorbike race.
b Some people find his jokes .... Unfortunately, I don't.
c Although my hotel was rather expensive, I decided that the prices were .... , considering the excellent service I had received.
d I found it hard to believe, but my sister was .... when she told me she was going to join the navy.
e His latest play has been .... by the critics.
f I am .... of my behaviour last night and am writing to you to apologise.
g I don't know why the baby started crying – he seemed .... when I put him to bed.
h My boss isn't here at the moment. His wife had to call for an ambulance when he was taken .... in the night.

Definitions

6 Match these words with the definitions below.

garish	prodigy	scepticism
priceless	sympathetic	portrait
colleague	scarce	

a Someone who is very gifted at a young age.
....
b A picture of a person. ....
c So expensive you cannot put a price on it.
....
d When there is very little of something.
....
e Too colourful. ....
f The state of not believing something.
....
g Used to describe someone who is very helpful or pleasant when you have problems.
....
h Someone who works with you.
....

PRICELESS OR WORTHLESS? 51

25 Urban decay, suburban hell

Reading

1 Read this article quickly, ignoring the missing sentences for the moment. Decide which of the descriptions below best summarises its content.

a A guide to amenities in the modern city
b The changing patterns in city lifestyles
c Opening hours for shopping in some cities

Time and the city

In modern cities, it is now time as much as space that separates urban functions, as people's lives are lived not only to different timetables, but also at wildly different rates. The mass timetable of the industrial city, with its factory sirens for the men at dawn and dusk, 9–5 office hours for the women and silent Sundays, has gone. In its place is flexi-time, part-time working, Sunday shopping and the 24-hour city.

European cities are responding to these changes perhaps faster than British cities. In at least half a dozen cities in Italy, for example, you will find the *Uffici Tempi* – the Offices of Time. What they do is to try to reorganise time more flexibly in the city, in order to meet new needs. ⬜1⬜ Usually located in the Mayor's office, the Uffici Tempi bring together transport providers, shop-owners, employers, trade unions, the police and other services, to see how their efforts might be better harmonised.

The main aim in all this is to increase the efficiency and productivity of the city. This can mean staggering starting times in schools, offices and factories to avoid rush hours, or shops opening later in the day but closing later too. ⬜2⬜

In a number of German cities, people are debating whether the timetable of the future city should be 6 × 6 or 4 × 9 – working hours, that is. ⬜3⬜ This would give them more time in the afternoons to be with children or to get the shopping.

In Britain, public leisure provision was one of the earliest sectors to respond to the need to adapt to changing time patterns. ⬜4⬜ The Oasis leisure centre in Swindon, from which the rock band took its name, has operated a 20-hour day, seven days a week for at least a decade.

⬜5⬜ After all, who likes working evenings or Sundays? Nevertheless, many city centres are now open for shopping seven days a week, and a number of them now promote themselves as '24-hour cities', where those with money can drink, eat, dance and even shop the whole night.

Time is flexible, but buildings aren't. ⬜6⬜ Adaptability has become the key skill. We are slowly abandoning the terminology of dormitory suburbs and industrial districts, in favour of mixed-use areas, out-of-town retailing and working from home. There is no doubt that planning theory is being challenged by the changing nature of time in the modern city.

52 UNIT 25

2 Now choose from the sentences A–G the one which fits each gap (1–6). There is one extra sentence which you do not need.

A One further benefit is that there can be more police about in the evening, patrolling the streets when people most need them.

B Apparently male workers favour a four-day week, while women workers, on the other hand, favour six shorter working days.

C The need for public services to adapt to our changing lifestyles has been quite difficult for some of the staff involved.

D This is particularly relevant for Italian women, an increasing number of whom have to balance two timetables, work and home.

E These timeshifts aren't always beneficial and can lead to conflict between households.

F It is interesting how often in modern consumer societies it is this industry which seems to anticipate or forecast social change.

G The mismatch between the fabric of the city and its uses, over time, is a serious architectural and planning problem.

3 Find words in the article to complete this table.

Verb	Noun
adapt	
	harmony
	location
produce	
	promotion
provide	
	response

Grammar

4 Match the two halves of these sentences and then say which ones are mixed conditionals.

1 If Carmen wasn't so rude,
2 If I had more space in this flat,
3 If you hadn't grabbed that waiter,
4 If we had booked the flight earlier,
5 If the council had gone ahead,
6 If they lived closer to us,

a we would still be waiting to order.
b I would have visited them.
c I would buy a grand piano.
d several people would be out of a job.
e I would have gone to her party.
f we would have got a good reduction.

G ····▸ STUDENT'S BOOK **page 207**

Vocabulary

5 Read the text opposite. Use the word given in capitals at the end of some of the lines to form a word that fits in the gap in the same line. There is an example at the beginning (0).

City centres are dynamic and change is (0) _unavoidable_ . **AVOID**
This is (1) .... true nowadays, when out-of-town **PARTICULAR**
complexes are threatening the (2) .... of shops **EXIST**
whose central (3) .... is no longer as attractive to **LOCATE**
the public. The (4) .... centres are the ones **SUCCEED**
which evolve to meet the different (5) .... of **REQUIRE**
their (6) .... In order to achieve this, the town **USE**
council may need to seek private (7) .... in the **INVEST**
(8) .... of its centre. Government help is, at the **GENERATE**
moment, (9) .... to be available, although this **LIKE**
policy may well be (10) .... in the future. **CONSIDER**

URBAN DECAY, SUBURBAN HELL

26 Getting around

Grammar

1 For questions 1–12, read the text below and think of the word which best fits each gap.
Use only **one** word in each gap.
There is an example at the beginning (0).

FAILINGS REVISITED

A few years ago, a government committee produced a major report (0) ......*on*...... transport and the environment. Now, just three years later, it has published (1) .... one. The first impression (2) .... reading the new report is that although (3) .... the first one we have witnessed significant changes, such (4) .... the end of the recession and the election of a new government, we still have the same problems outlined in the original report. These include high levels of traffic growth and rising concentrations of nitrogen dioxides.

Nevertheless, some positive changes (5) .... occur over the period: there now appears to (6) .... widespread recognition of the importance of public transport, and car manufacturers have been paying (7) .... attention to fuel consumption than before. However, any gains in this area are being cancelled out (8) .... other factors. According to the report, Britain (9) .... adopt changes in behaviour to stop damaging trends in transport. The report welcomes the new government's move to establish a closer relationship (10) .... transport and land use policies, but argues that local authorities are (11) .... thinking ahead to the creation of integrated transport systems in the long-term. Will there be a need in three years' time (12) .... a further report on why things have stayed the same? Let us hope not.

2 Complete the second sentence so that it has a similar meaning to the first sentence, using the word given. Do not change the word given. You must use between two and five words, including the word given.

1 Pedestrians' lives are endangered by speeding motorists.
risk
Pedestrians' lives .... by speeding motorists.

2 Hydrofoils are popular and can go at high speeds because of their aerodynamic fins.
whose
Hydrofoils, ... them to go at high speeds, are popular.

3 The true price of using our cars has not been successfully communicated by the government.
message
The government has been unsuccessful in
....
about the true price of using our cars.

4 Planned changes in traffic routing are designed for local people, who will benefit enormously.
whom
Local people, ...
change traffic routing are designed,
will benefit enormously.

5 We should do this quickly, as it might hurt!
get
Let's ....
quickly, as it might hurt!

G ⋯▶ STUDENT'S BOOK **page 208**

Writing

4 Correct the fifteen spelling errors in this report on the dangers of swimming near Whittisham Beach.

Vocabulary

3 Answer these questions, choosing the best answer A, B or C. Look up any words you don't know in your dictionary.

1 What comes out of a car exhaust?
A clouds B fumes C scents
2 A funnel is on a ship, but where else can you use one?
A in a lab B in a garden C in a bedroom
3 Planes have flaps on their wings, but what is a cat flap?
A a large cat collar B an angry group of cats
C an entrance for cats
4 If you are 'up the creek without a paddle', how are you?
A soaking wet B in difficulty
C far from home
5 What do you use to operate the gearbox in America?
A a gear lever B a gear stick C a gearshift
6 Where else might you find a cabin, apart from on a ship?
A in a forest B at a swimming pool
C on a wall
7 What will you **not** find on a dashboard?
A switches B dials C slots
8 Which of these words has to be changed to make the verb form? What is this verb?
A flap B radiator C brake

Introduction
I have been asked to investigate the dangers to swimers who use Whittisham Beach. There have been severeal incidents recently, due to increased use of the sea by jetskis and speedboats.

The dangers
Jetskis, whose top speeds are in exces of 100kph, come in far to close to the shore. As people who swim have their faces under water, they do not neccesarily see or hear them approaching. Children's lifes are expecially endangered, as they are less easy to see. Untill jetskis are baned, people will continue to be put at risk.

I was also informed of an accident involveing a windsurfer, whose bored was hit by a motorboat 200 metres out to sea. Fortunatelly, there was no injury to the people involved, but if the motorboat had been going at full speed, the situation would have been much worse.

Recommendation
I beleive Whittisham Council should take urgent action about this. In the short term, notices warning people of the dangers should be placed at both ends of the beach. Of equally high priorite, councillors must introduce a new policy to limit the use of jetskis and other pleazur craft to a safe distance from the beach.

GETTING AROUND

27 Material girl

Reading

1 You are going to read an article about how bodyguards are trained. Seven sentences have been removed from the article. Choose from the sentences A–H the one which fits each gap (1–7). There is one extra sentence which you do not need to use.

LOOKING AFTER THE RICH AND FAMOUS

'A properly trained bodyguard will constantly be on the alert, looking for anything that strikes them as suspicious,' says Peter Consterdine, a Black Belt 7th Dan karate expert and former Special Forces soldier who trains bodyguards.

Today's bodyguards are educated, intelligent, and trained in advanced surveillance techniques, fighting, driving, first aid and anti-terrorist devices. These sophisticated 'Grey Men' take on a variety of roles. **1** ☐ This is because a potential assailant who spots you as security will see how your protection system works and get round it.

Clients can come from all walks of life, and the security agencies are reporting a growing number of inquiries. Not just from VIPs and celebrity figures, but also from top businessmen and captains of industry. **2** ☐

If you like the sound of being a bodyguard, there are various training courses on offer. **3** ☐ The key organisations train students up to an operational level. After a two-day induction course, you'll undergo an intensive week of serious training. You need to be pretty fit beforehand, as physical training – some heavy going – is always involved.

Students are taught how to 'ghost' and 'shield' to protect their client from all kinds of attack, no matter how trivial. You'll learn how to deal calmly with threatening situations, make safety assessments and avoid risky environments. **4** ☐ You will then be put through similar scenarios and marked for performance. Your task is to prevent, rather than deter, an attack.

Ex-SAS trooper Jim Short is director general of the International Bodyguard Association. 'It's important for the Grey Man or Woman to spot a potential threat and deal with it without anyone noticing,' he says. 'There is little point in having a gang of big, well-built men around a client in a sensitive situation.' **5** ☐

There are situations, however, when people will deliberately use large minders to attract attention. The classic case is Madonna. When she went jogging in London she took 10 massive minders. **6** ☐

Short thoroughly checks out all applicants' past histories. **7** ☐ 'It only comes with experience and continual training.' Bodyguards must be ready to travel anywhere at very short notice. The pay is good, but contracts are usually short-term, and can last from a few hours to six months. Conditions vary, but bodyguards need to be prepared for any eventuality and have the wardrobe to match!

A They are simply going to attract too much attention.

B But they can be expensive, and there are no guarantees of finding work afterwards.

C For instance, if your client's a rock star, you act and dress like part of the band; if it's a VIP, you need a shirt and tie.

D What happened? Instant media coverage.

E After a series of lectures and presentations, qualified bodyguards give practical demonstrations.

F One time my boss was targeted by a gang of kidnappers.

G These people often hire personal 'minders' for their wives and daughters.

H They're told right at the start that they cannot become a bodyguard overnight.

56 UNIT 27

Vocabulary

2 Below are some phrases taken from the article. Use each one once only, in its correct form, in sentences a–f.

| to look for | to take on | to get round |
| to deal with | to protect from | little/no point in |

a There's .... going to the party too early – no one will be there.

b I was .... a new job when I saw an ad in one of the trade papers.

c Many famous pop singers .... the tax laws in their countries.

d Nowadays, singers need to be .... some of their more enthusiastic fans.

e A good Public Relations firm will .... any difficult incidents when you're rich and famous.

f I .... the job of looking after my younger sister after school.

3 Using one of the prepositions in the box, fill the gaps in sentences a–g below.

| for | after | at | on | in | between | of |

a She was responsible .... looking .... her younger brothers and sisters.

b Peter's really made a great success .... his new career.

c Actors need to believe .... what they are doing in order to be convincing.

d I'm just not very good .... singing.

e Andy Warhol said everyone can be famous .... fifteen minutes.

f Congratulations .... being the first person to ring in with the right answer!

g I found it difficult to choose .... dancing and acting.

Grammar

4 Read the essay below and rewrite it so that it is grammatically correct.

Famous Latin American Pop Singers

In Mexico you will find much different types of music: traditional, mariachi, boleros, etc. But the type which young peoples prefer is the pop-rock. Most of the records they like are about love, their experiences and of course, the problems they see them in society or in the world. The most famous pop singer is Luis Miguel, which has now made many albums. There are also many of women who are famous in our music business. One of them is Shakira and she is one of the best female singer and she also write his own songs.

Gloria Estefan is internationally famous and she holds an especial place in Mexican pop music, even she is from the Cuba, not Mexico. Gloria went to Miami after the Cuban revolution in 1961. In 1975 she sang lot songs at a wedding. There she met with Emilio Estefan, leader of a band which called The Miami Latin Boys. Soon the band has changed his name to The Miami Sound Machine and by 1983, the group was well known all Central and South America. In 1993 Gloria decided to explore her Cuban musical heritage with an album called 'Mi Tierra'. She was chosen for to sing the official theme song of the 1996 Summer Olympics, 'Reach'.

28 Sense and sensitivity

Vocabulary

1 Try this questionnaire from an in-flight magazine on the colour blue.

1 If something happens once in a blue moon, how often does it happen?
   a   never
   b   rarely
   c   once in a lifetime

2 The super-computer Deeper Blue beat someone at which game?
   a   Scrabble
   b   chess
   c   Monopoly

3 What computer corporation is known as 'Big Blue'?
   a   IBM
   b   Apple
   c   Packard-Bell

4 When a ship flies the 'Blue Peter', what is it doing?
   a   leaving port
   b   carrying dangerous materials
   c   signalling an emergency

5 In what country is 'G'day, Blue' a traditional greeting?
   a   New Zealand
   b   Canada
   c   Australia

2 For questions 1–12, read the text below and think of the word which best fits each gap. Use only one word in each gap. There is an example at the beginning (0).

What colour car do you drive?

Shy? Introverted? Suffering from depression and do not know why? Well, now **(0)** ..*there*... is a simple cure – change the colour of your car.

Unlikely though it may seem, psychologists have determined character traits associated with the colour of vehicles. Owners of pastel-coloured cars **(1)** .... as lilac, lime and beige are eight **(2)** .... more likely to have suffered depression than people driving blue **(3)** .... silver ones. They are also more likely to have **(4)** .... a victim of road rage abuse in **(5)** .... last year.

'Choice of car colour says more **(6)** .... someone's personality than the clothes they wear or the house they live in,' says Conrad King, consultant psychologist for the RAC*, the organisation **(7)** .... commissioned the survey of 1,000 people. 'Colour preferences can indicate a definite psychosocial pecking order on the roads, **(8)** .... the owners of black and red cars struggling **(9)** .... the dominant position. We were totally surprised. We had been under the impression that colour was just a haphazard choice. But society is changing and this change is reflected, **(10)** .... some extent, by the colour of the cars people drive.' **(11)** .... the most popular car colours are red and blue, white and green are **(12)** .... far behind and silver is now being seen as the most fashionable.

* Royal Automobile Club: an association for drivers in Britain

UNIT 28

3   Read this extract from an article to find out what your choice of car colour says about your personality. Change the words in brackets to form a word which fits in the sentence.
    There is an example at the beginning (0).

    BLACK
    First choice for success-driven and (0) <u>ambitious</u> (ambition) drivers.

    RED
    Outgoing and (1) .... (impulse) people. They are easily (2) .... (boredom) and prefer spontaneity and (3) .... (create).

    SILVER
    Associated with style and finesse. Can tend towards the pompous.

    WHITE
    These people are (4) .... (distance), (5) .... (duty) and methodical.

    GREY
    (6) .... (safety) and (7) .... (caution) drivers choose this colour.

    BLUE
    These drivers are team players, (8) .... (society) but lacking in (9) .... (imagine).

    GREEN
    Usually drivers who are class conscious and (10) .... (tradition) in outlook.

    PASTEL
    Avoid this colour as the drivers can easily get (11) .... (depression).

Grammar

4   These definitions all refer to plural words. Write down the words.

    a Women wear them on their legs in winter. T _ _ _ _ _
    b You need them to see things a long way away. B _ _ _ _ _ _ _ _ _
    c You cut things with these. S _ _ _ _ _ _ _
    d You can wear these in bed. P _ _ _ _ _ _
    e I need mine to watch a film. G _ _ _ _ _ _

    These definitions all refer to singular words. Write down the words.

    f Doing the javelin and the long-jump. A _ _ _ _ _ _ _ _

    g Learning about equations. M _ _ _ _ _ _ _ _ _ _
    h Journalists report this. N _ _ _
    i The study of how government works. P _ _ _ _ _ _ _
    j The science of light, fission and fusion. P _ _ _ _ _ _

    G ⋯ STUDENT'S BOOK page 208

Writing

5   Below is an informal letter. Join the words so that they make grammatically accurate sentences. Use all the words given and add any extra that you think are needed. Do not change the order of the words.

    EXAMPLE: *I / happy / hear / you / good holiday / Scotland.*
    I am/was happy to hear that you had a good holiday in Scotland.

    Dear Freda,

    Thank / letter. I / please / your news / be / better than / last time / you write / me. Both my parents send / love.

    Last week I / buy / new jeans / new shop / centre / town. Staff / be / very helpful. I / have to / try on / eight different pairs / the majority / be / too tight or / right colour.

    jeans /cost / ninety pounds / I think / not be / too dear / good quality ones. Everybody I know / wear / designer jeans / my parents / think / crazy. Neither my father / my mother / be interested / fashion. All / my mother's clothes / be dark blue. I wish / she wear / different colour sometimes!

    The real reason / write / invite you / my birthday party / next week. A group of us / go / new club. Would you / come? / Ring / soon.

    Give my regards / family. I hope / well.

    Love,

    Camilla

6   Now write a paragraph. Say how you feel about different colours and explain how colours are used in expressions in your own language.

29 Newshounds

Reading

1 You are going to read a newspaper article about government policy and television. First, check your understanding of the words and phrases below by matching them to their definitions a–e. All these words occur in the article which follows.

1 elitism
2 government initiatives
3 indoctrination
4 phenomenon
5 soap opera

a official action to solve a problem
b a television drama serial about daily life
c something that is observed to happen or exist
d the belief that one section of society is superior
e forcing particular ideas on people

2 Now read the article. For questions 1–8, choose the answer (A, B, C or D) which you think fits best according to the article.

EastEnders, a BBC soap opera

The Minister of Education was interviewed on the radio last week about his plans for raising reading standards. He talked about the need to reach a wider public, speaking enthusiastically about new
7 ways to achieve this, such as by advertising on television, by handing out books to babies at their nine-month health checks, and, most significantly, through the cooperation of three leading television soap opera producers, who have been persuaded to weave into the plot the message that reading is good for you. There was no mistaking the radio interviewer's disapproval – soap operas tailoring their storylines to government initiatives? 'Indoctrination,' he muttered.

Television, however, is the obvious place to go in search of lost readers. There is hardly much point using the public library or the local bookshop to promote reading, as those who don't read rarely enter either, and probably associate both with the school classroom, and consequently with activities which are boring. Today, whether we like it or not, film and television are the point of entry for large numbers of people into the delights of storytelling and the appreciation of a good plot. Think how many people have bought copies of the 'book of the TV drama'. This phenomenon took one nineteenth-century novel to number one in the bestsellers' list recently.

When I was a student in the 1960s, I was taught that popular culture – pulp fiction and romance – manipulated the working classes, persuading them to be obedient to those above them, making them want less in life and be happy with second best. Now, I believe that argument was a piece of appalling elitism. All those who consume popular culture know exactly what its effect on them is. In our media-aware society, each of us makes a decision whether to 'buy in' and join the crowd, or stay out and be different.

Soap operas are the place where huge numbers of adults and young people alike tap into the common concerns of everyday life. Day-time viewers turn to them for companionship, treating every desperate choice to be made by the characters as their own. The popularity of an individual programme depends on the script-writers catching the mood of the general public. Plots are tightly steered towards the things we care about, from the trivial ups and downs of our personal relationships to the shame of domestic violence.

Of course, there is always the danger that those in authority might try to take over our minds via our favourite forms of entertainment. But I think we can rely on the fact that political messages, however cleverly put across, always appear bossy and aggressive. That's why we usually vote with our feet during a party political broadcast, whatever the party. The joy of fiction, on the other hand – and a soap is, after all, a form of modern fiction – is that it is bound to adapt its 'public information' material, in order to create emotional intensity, pace and drama. Under these conditions, indoctrination cannot occur. When the soap opera *Coronation Street* shows a father who dropped out of school being caught off guard by his five-year-old son, unable to read his bedtime story book, nobody watching is being forced to enrol in adult reading classes. But if a few dads recognise that they are not alone in having to memorise the text of a favourite story so as to keep their child's respect, so much the better.

1 What does 'this' refer to in line 7?
   A raising reading standards
   B reaching a wider public
   C giving books to babies
   D working with TV producers

2 Using a library to encourage reading is ineffective because
   A people prefer to go to bookshops.
   B it reminds people of being at school.
   C people find library activities boring.
   D it fails to get to the right people.

3 One effect of television is that it
   A attracts a lot more viewers than previously.
   B makes people watch things they don't enjoy.
   C encourages people to write their own stories.
   D increases the sales of some related books.

4 What was the writer told about popular culture as a student?
   A It reduced certain people's expectations.
   B It was a bad influence on the whole of society.
   C It discouraged people from working hard.
   D It made the lower classes too argumentative.

5 According to the writer, some people watch soap operas because they
   A help them to make their own decisions.
   B know they can depend on the plots.
   C prevent them from feeling too lonely.
   D can talk about them with other people.

6 How does a soap opera achieve success?
   A by accurately reflecting people's thoughts and feelings
   B through the inclusion of violent and shocking scenes
   C by using a number of different script-writers
   D through careful control of the final recordings

7 Why does the writer say that indoctrination cannot occur in soap operas?
   A They do not put across political messages well.
   B There is not enough time to include any argument.
   C There is no direct attempt to tell people what to do.
   D They cannot change the information to fit the drama.

8 What would be the best title for this article?
   A How to develop a successful storyline
   B The role of television drama in reading
   C New government funding for soap operas
   D What is bad about popular culture today

Vocabulary

English idioms

3 Fill in the missing words in the sentences to complete the idioms about parts of the body.

   a I'm just about .... above water, but I desperately need the new research assistant I was promised.

   b New students at the college never take very long to find ....

   c Governments have .... to these atrocities for far too long; it's time for action to be taken.

   d Celebrities on TV chat shows often have .... in a discussion, because of their popularity with the live audience.

   e Many companies got .... when the Russian economy collapsed.

   f Keith, I don't often see .... you, but I think you're absolutely right this time.

   g Copernicus .... existing theory on .... when he suggested, rightly, that the planets go round the sun.

   h Julie got .... at the last minute and decided not to go through with the wedding.

4 The fifteen words in this wordsearch are all part of idioms in this unit. Words can be horizontal, vertical or diagonal. They may run forwards or backwards. Find them and then give the complete idioms.

T	R	I	D	O	P	I	E
L	G	W	T	A	R	C	N
E	U	C	O	R	E	I	D
B	A	P	S	W	I	N	G
G	R	I	P	S	X	G	L
A	D	S	T	O	R	M	O
C	O	W	I	N	D	O	W
T	H	I	N	M	I	C	E

30 Anything for a laugh

Vocabulary

1 For questions 1–10, read the text below. Use the word in capitals at the end of some of the lines to form a word that fits in the gap in the same line. There is an example at the beginning (0).

Comedians Russell Brand and Lenny Henry

Red Nose Day

Red Nose Day is one of Britain's most **(0)** ...successful... events, which raises a huge amount of money for good causes. It is organised by the charity Comic Relief and takes place in March. Many well-known **(1)** .... take part, as well as actors, **(2)** .... , TV personalities and other celebrities. All these people in the public eye bravely take on **(3)** .... challenges, from learning to sing to sitting in a bath full of cold baked beans!

In addition to a great evening's **(4)** .... on TV on the day itself, there is a wide **(5)** .... of programmes and live events in the weeks leading up to Red Nose Day. At schools and colleges, students do silly things for cash and many workplaces organise **(6)** .... money-raising stunts. Shops and supermarkets sell the famous red noses and other **(7)** .... , such as red hair dye and badges.

Through short documentary films, TV **(8)** .... learn how the money raised in previous years has helped Comic Relief to make a real **(9)** .... to people in need, both in Britain and in Africa. Some of the stories shown are shocking, but the message is always a positive one and there are many happy **(10)** .... It is extremely moving to see how people's lives can be changed. Comic Relief has been able to achieve a great deal by making people laugh.

SUCCEED

COMEDY
MUSIC
USUAL

ENTERTAIN
VARY

SAME
PRODUCE

VIEW

DIFFERENT

END

2 How many words for 'funny' do you know?
Complete the words below and then use them in sentences a–c.

1 H __ L __ __ __ __ __ S   3 W __ __ __ Y
2 __ M __ __ __ G   4 C __ __ __ C

a Satire, which makes fun of politics and current affairs, is often a dry, ... form of entertainment.

b .... strips are .... for adults and children alike.

c His .... jokes had us doubled up with laughter.

UNIT 30

3 Fill in the missing words in these jokes to do with crime.

   a Don't you know that crime doesn't ……………… ?
   – I know, but the hours are good.

   b Order, order in the ……………………… !
   – Thank you, Judge. I'll take a ham and cheese on rye bread.

   c He went to jail for something he didn't do – he didn't ……………………… his taxes!

   d This is the fifth time you've ……………………… before me. I fine you ten dollars.
   – Your Honour, don't I get a discount for being a ……………………… customer?

   e Are you guilty or ……………………… guilty?
   – That seems a rather personal question, Judge!

Grammar

4 Complete the second sentence so that it has a similar meaning to the first sentence, using the word given. **Do not change the word given. You must use between two and five words, including the word given.**

   1 How can you stand these tasteless jokes?
   put
   How can you ……………………… of these jokes?

   2 I prefer to go out to clubs and see live comedy instead of watching TV recordings of it.
   than
   I prefer to see live comedy
   ………………………
   watching TV recordings of it.

   3 The flight attendant told us to extinguish all cigarettes in preparation for landing.
   out
   We were told by the flight attendant to
   ………………………
   the plane was preparing to land.

   4 The customs officer demanded to know what was in his suitcase.
   insisted
   The customs officer
   ……………………… of his suitcase.

   5 His boss told him he was fired and ordered him to leave immediately.
   got
   His boss told him he
   ………………………
   and said he should leave immediately.

   6 I'd prefer to get going now, before it gets dark.
   rather
   I ……………………… until it gets dark, so I'll get going now.

ANYTHING FOR A LAUGH   63

Answer key

Unit 1

Vocabulary

Spellcheck

1 hairstyle; outrageous; jewellery (or 'jewelry' in US English); bracelets; earrings; expensive; exciting; suits; fashion-conscious; different

2 a imagine   e According … writer
   b beautiful   f apologise
   c brilliant   g disappointed
   d beginning   h Happiness

Phrasal verbs

3 a keep up with
   b threw on
   c get away with; smarten … up
   d dressed up; stood out

Reading

4 They date from 1886.

5 a False – there is one other pair, according to the text
   b False – (paid even more for)
   c True – the company historian
   d False – they have a leather patch
   e True
   f True

6 oldest; the most expensive; the highest; the most important

7 a excessive   b ordinary   c appropriately
   d delighted   e frayed   f remarkably

Grammar

Comparatives

8 b are more comfortable than
   c are more casual than
   d are thinner than
   e is younger than
   f is bigger than
   g is less dangerous than
   h is more/less tiring than (!)

9 a not as cheap as
   b not as difficult as
   c not as fast as

Unit 2

Reading

1 board games

2 a appreciate
   b working out problems
   c chance
   d business
   e interrupting
   f keen
   g plonk
   h limit

Grammar

Present tenses

3 *Suggested verbs*
   a5 says; are rising
   b1 believe; offer
   c3 are spending; means
   d4 are stopping; think
   e2 seem; involve

4 1 know   2 like   3 keeps
   4 realises/knows 5 forgets/hates   6 hate
   7 likes   8 sounds   9 understands
   10 wish

Vocabulary

5 Vertical word: Internet

   1 graphics   2 clone   3 adventure
   4 opponent   5 version   6 weapons
   7 solve   8 effects

6 a anti-social
   b popular
   c demanding
   d aggressive
   e sophisticated

ANSWER KEY 65

7 **The Internet:** browsing, access, downloading, surf the web, file, submit
Computers: back-up, interface, upgrade, file
Video games: sound effects, graphics, clone, interface

Unit 3
Vocabulary
Prepositions

1 1 off   2 in   3 on
   4 on   5 at   6 across/along
   7 across/around 8 on   9 in
   10 into   11 to   12 onto/to

Travel quiz

2 a cruise   b sightseers   c ferry
   d courier   e caravans   f crossing
   g cabin

Writing
Phrasal verbs

3 1 g   2 f   3 b   4 e
   5 h   6 a   7 c   8 d

4 a feel like   b depart   c put up with
   d ring up   e recovering f continue

5 a Formal written
   b Informal written
   c Formal written
   d Formal spoken
   e Informal spoken
   f Formal spoken
   g Formal written
   h Informal/semi-formal written
   i Informal spoken
   j Informal spoken

Grammar
Obligation, necessity, permission

6 a have to/must
   b have to/must
   c don't have to
   d need to
   e let
   f had to
   g needn't have
   h isn't permitted

Unit 4
Reading
Guessing unknown words

3 a going towards
   b no longer used
   c check/look for
   d had been dropped all over (in the way that litter is dropped, i.e. randomly)
   e saw
   f where bears can't get in
   g covered in pieces of wood to prevent entry (a *board* is a piece of wood)
   h looking round carefully
   i the place where food is kept in a kitchen
   j fixed, without looking away at all (*glue* is something you use to stick things together)

4 a F   b T   c T   d F   e F
   f F   g T   h F   i F

5 the old railway building; the bear

Grammar
as and *like*

6 a as (well) as
   b like
   c like
   d as
   e as
   f as
   g like

Compound adjectives

7 a duty-free
   b cross-eyed
   c long-distance
   d absent-minded
   e hand-made
   f first-class
   g second-class/second-hand
   h self-catering/self-made
   i right-handed/right-hand/right-minded

8 a hand-made/second-hand
   b long-distance
   c second-hand
   d cross-eyed/absent-minded
   e duty-free
   f first-class
   g self-catering

Unit 5
Vocabulary

1.
    1. disaster
    2. compensation
    3. dreadful
    4. earlier
    5. worse
    6. unhelpful
    7. worried
    8. opposite
    9. surprised
    10. thought
    11. meant
    12. spend
    13. conditions
    14. stiff
    15. refund

Grammar
Past tenses

2.

Infinitive	Past tense	Past participle
find	found	found
flee	fled	fled
grab	grabbed	grabbed
hold	held	held
keep	kept	kept
realise	realised	realised
sink	sank	sunk
swerve	swerved	swerved
try	tried	tried
wave	waved	waved

3.
    1. saw
    2. knew
    3. had taken
    4. tried
    5. happened
    6. went
    7. realised
    8. had interfered

Suggested endings

a The cliff was getting nearer and nearer, so Harry threw himself out of the window and landed on the ground, unharmed. The car went over the cliff.

b He swerved into a field on his left and noticed the largest pile of hay he had ever seen. He thought quickly. He drove into the haystack and thankfully survived.

c Harry went to pieces and was screaming and shouting as the car went over the cliff. It landed two hundred metres below and burst into flames, with Harry inside.

Reading
4. 1 D 2 A 3 D 4 A
   5 B 6 C 7/8 A/C (*in any order*)

Unit 6
Reading
1 He has just won £12.3m on the National Lottery.

2. 1 E 2 B 3 D 4 C

Grammar
3.
    a hadn't bought
    b claims
    c offered
    d phones
    e grabbed
    f hadn't been
    g wasn't/weren't
    h ended up

4.
    a Lottery winners usually …
    b I seldom have …
    c People are always telling me …
    d I never worried …
    e I'm often scared stiff …
    f He's normally here …

5
1 if you don't leave
2 usually in control of
3 (just) in case I (ever)
4 never miss (watching)
5 had a sleepless night/had no sleep/had a night without sleep
6 able to take in

Vocabulary

6 a prize (not part of bank set); nouns
b give (not receiving); verbs
c delight (pleasant feeling); nouns
d suspicious (different emotion); adjectives
e take off (different meaning – not to do with solving problems); phrasal verbs

Unit 7
Reading

1 She enjoyed it.

2 a 193 kph
b She was worried about going out in a powerboat.
c Because it is so dangerous – there is a danger of fire and crashing.
d No, you can use them for recreation as well.
e No.

3 a went faster than
b terrifying
c the place where the driver sits
d material which stops fire burning you so quickly
e leisure

4 1 C   2 E   3 A   4 F   5 D

Grammar
Gerunds and infinitives

5 a Jenny suggested going to the party in a taxi.
b I look forward to hearing from you in the near future.
c I don't mind doing it.
d I'm interested in learning Spanish.
e Correct
f I'll help you with your homework when I finish writing my letter.
g I am used to doing the washing up.
h Correct
i Correct
j I'm going to town to buy a new jumper.
k I object to paying to park my car.
l I can't afford to lend you any more money.
m Correct

Vocabulary

6 a win
b nil
c referee
d court
e clubs
f give
g laps

Writing

7 Punctuated story:

> It was the greatest day of my life. I had been picked to play for my national football team and now we were playing in the finals of the World Cup. All of us waited nervously in the changing rooms, then all of a sudden it was time. We ran through the door and into the tunnel leading to the pitch. A wall of noise hit us. The fans were all on their feet, cheering and shouting. I felt so proud.
>
> The whistle blew and the match began. An opportunity came and I took it. I could see Pele and Cantona in the stands, shouting, 'Go on, you can do it!' So, with one great kick, I scored a goal. All the other players came over to congratulate me and hug me. I heard them saying, 'Come on. It's time to wake up!' It was a woman's voice. 'I didn't know there were any women in our team,' I said to myself, and at that moment I woke up and heard my doctor telling me I would make a full recovery.

Unit 8
Vocabulary

1
- a architect
- b robber
- c psychiatrist
- d model
- e cashier
- f plumber
- g head
- h surgeon
- i courier
- j captain
- k vet
- l warder

3
- a got the sack
- b profession
- c do overtime
- d employer
- e flexi-time
- f unemployed

4
- 1 D
- 2 B
- 3 B
- 4 A
- 5 B
- 6 C
- 7 A
- 8 C
- 9 D
- 10 D

Grammar
used to and *would*

5
- 1 used to do / did
- 2 found
- 3 discovered
- 4 included
- 5 used to spend, would spend, spent
- 6 used to use, would use, used
- 7 confirmed
- 8 used to be, was
- 9 used to take, would take, took
- 10 used to be, were
- 11 used to walk, would walk, walked
- 12 used to be, were
- 13 used to visit, would visit, visited
- 14 estimated

Unit 9
Reading

1 It is giving them misleading information on product packaging.

2
- 1 E
- 2 G
- 3 A
- 4 D
- 5 F
- 6 B

3
- a regulations; rules; code; verdict
- b letting ... down; brought out; get away with

Grammar
Modals

4
- a could/might
- b must
- c can't
- d can't/couldn't
- e must
- f could/might

5
- 1 to
- 2 it
- 3 the
- 4 were
- 5 spite
- 6 not
- 7 is/was
- 8 must
- 9 a
- 10 that
- 11 which/that
- 12 could/might

Vocabulary

6 c, f and h do not collocate with *broad*; *deep* could be used instead.

7 **a** jingle
b slogan
c budget
d impact
e brand

Unit 10
Vocabulary

1 1 C   2 B   3 A   4 D
   5 A   6 D   7 C   8 A
   9 C   10 C   11 C   12 B

Phrasal verbs

2 **a** take off
b turn out
c get on
d set up
e end up
f run out
1 had taken off
2 will end up
3 are turning out
4 will (have) run out / are going to run out
5 will be set up / is going to be set up
6 are you getting on

Grammar
Future tenses

3 *Suggested answers*

a Within 20 years, manned spacecraft will have landed on Mars.
b In the 22nd century, it may be possible to launch starships, whose destination would be other galaxies.
c Soon, people will be able to travel to low orbit and the journey time between Europe and New Zealand will be only an hour.

4 *Suggested answer*

Between 10 and 12 January, 2012, Elwood College of Technology is hosting a conference on future developments in space. Guest speakers will include science fiction writer John T. Price and leading scientist Professor Paul Rhodes, who will be speaking about his latest research into alien lifeforms.

Unit 11
Vocabulary

1 1 mentally
   2 attraction
   3 personality
   4 appearance
   5 likely
   6 extension
   7 possibly
   8 choice
   9 social
  10 reasonable

2 **a** nervous   afraid   terrified   petrified
b pleased   thrilled/delighted   overjoyed
c disappointed   unhappy   miserable/depressed
d interested   keen   fascinated   obsessed
e surprised   astonished   speechless   incredulous
f attractive   lovely   beautiful   stunning
g plain   unattractive   ugly   revolting

American English

3 I think I was very privileged
I really loved
On the underground
She got/became really embarrassed

4 1 g   2 f   3 k   4 i
   5 j   6 b   7 e   8 h
   9 a   10 c   11 d

Writing

5 Corrections are shown in bold.

Dear Jody,

Thanks for your letter; it was good to **hear** from you. You'll be pleased **to know** that I've found someone to **share** the flat with. She's called Elena Richmann and she's **an** actress from Canada. I interviewed about 20 people before I **saw** her. She's very **nice** and we really get on well together. Let me **tell** you a bit about her. She's about 1m 52cm in **height** and has short, black, curly hair; in fact she **looks** a bit like your sister! She's incredibly **lively** so she should be fun to have around. We're both interested **in** the same type of films and we seem to have similar tastes **in** music. She hates **cooking** so I won't have to **worry** about having a messy kitchen!

One drawback is that, when she **is** making a movie, she needs **to get** up really early, about 4.30 in the morning, to go to the set to get her make-up and costume sorted out. She says she'll be really **quiet**, so we'll have to see. Anyway, I haven't **noticed any** bad habits yet! You **must meet** her – why don't you come over to the flat next **Saturday** and we can have a meal together? Drop me a line to let me know.

Love

Tanya

6 *Suggested answer*

> Dear Lynne,
>
> I thought I'd write and tell you all my latest news. We've got new neighbours. You remember I told you that we had a large family living next door? Well, the father has got a new job in New York and they moved out last week. They were quite fun, but a bit noisy. I particularly got fed up with the two children – there was a boy of about one and a girl aged four. They used to scream a lot, especially when their dog, Blackie, used to jump up at them. Their parents and their grandpa and grandma were nice though.
>
> The new neighbours are a family with identical twin girls, aged nine. They are very pretty and, so far, seem quite sweet and friendly. I hope I will be able to tell them apart. Their Dad came over yesterday to say 'hello' and we're going to have them all over for a barbecue next weekend. I'll write and let you know if my first impressions of them were right!
>
> That's all my news for now. Hope you're keeping well.
>
> Best wishes

Unit 12
Reading
1 1 D 2 C 3 B 4 A 5 D
      6 B 7 D

Grammar
2 a I had to be trained by the manager.
   b Usually cuckoo clocks are made out of wood.
   c The science exhibition will be visited by many people.
   d My camera was stolen on the bus.
   e He had his bike stolen.
   f It has been proved that water freezes at 0 degrees C.
   g French is spoken here.
   h Many designs have been made for new planes.
   i The house is being painted at the moment.
   j The car is being cleaned.
   k Maria was born in April.
   l A jet is flown by Hamid every day.
   m They were asked to a party.
   n Today's meeting is cancelled / has been cancelled.
   o My house was built last year.
   p I was hurt in a road accident.

Vocabulary
3 1 D 2 A 3 C 4 B 5 B 6 A

Phrasal verbs with *come* and *take*
4 a inherited
   b resembles
   c started (a new hobby)
   d regain consciousness
   e running
   f face/meet
   g like
   h produce
   i understand/absorb
   j found/discovered (by chance)
   k accepting/getting

Unit 13
Reading
2 1 E 2 G 3 C 4 A 5 D 6 F

Grammar
3 a Zeinaida said she had gone to the local paper and had told them their plans. They had asked her some questions to check her out, but in the end they had promised to run the story.

   b Chris Searle said that that morning he had gone in through the side entrance. The school secretary had been handing out the registers as normal, but there couldn't have been more than 20 or 30 kids in the whole building.

   c The pupil said that while they had been outside the gates, teachers had come across and (had) talked to them. Some had been sympathetic, though they hadn't been able to admit it. Some had been aggressive and had thrown gym shoes at them.

   d Chris Searle said that those children had been made to feel that being ordinary meant failure. But he argued that it is the ordinary people and their daily work that make a country. (*Present tense is used as this is an ongoing truth.*)

Vocabulary
4 1 made a good impression
   2 make sense of
   3 made use of
   4 made their move
   5 made their feelings known

5 a make   f go on / start
    b had   g take … make
    c made   h take
    d do   i made
    e made   j makes/made

Unit 14
Grammar

1 1 in   7 much/many
    2 be   8 made/did
    3 a/one   9 through
    4 the   10 lots/plenty
    5 with   11 when
    6 his   12 been

Writing

2 h; d; g; b; i; a; c; f; e

> As a child, Tom Gardiner had always known that he would be rich. At 19, he had set up his own software company, and it soon took off in a big way. When the company made record profits last June, Tom celebrated in style, by throwing a huge party on board his magnificent yacht. The whole event cost nearly a million pounds, with the bill for flowers alone equivalent to the yearly salary of one of his programmers. This year, it had been expected that Tom's company would perform even better. But recently, unimaginable things have been going wrong. For instance, many customers have had to return faulty software. There have also been reports of a strange virus in some products, which causes a computer screen to go orange and then flash up the message 'Tom is sinking'. It seems that one particularly discontented employee has attempted to programme bankruptcy for Tom's company. Even if the company survives, Tom has been given a clear warning, which he cannot afford to ignore.

Vocabulary

4 1 selection
    2 individually
    3 specialise
    4 successful
    5 availability
    6 underdeveloped
    7 imaginative
    8 unusual
    9 digging
    10 expansion

5 a all in all
    b all very well
    c of all
    d for all
    e after all
    f all in

6 *Both:* overheads; grant; earnings; income
    Only of people: salary; wages; redundancy; unemployment benefit
    Only of companies: revenue; profits; takings

Unit 15
Vocabulary

1 1 B   2 D   3 A   4 B   5 A
    6 D   7 A   8 B   9 C   10 A

2 a recycled
    b extinct
    c second-hand
    d drought
    e floods
    f flash
    g shower

Writing

3 1 As
    2 Despite
    3 when
    4 Besides
    5 So
    6 Although
    7 because/as a result
    8 as a result
    9 though
    10 Furthermore

Grammar

some, any, no, every

5 a anything/something
    b anyone/anybody
    c everywhere
    d No one/Nobody
    e something
    f anywhere
    g nothing
    h Everyone/Everybody
    i anything

Unit 16
Reading
1
- 1 C
- 2/3 B/E *(in any order)*
- 4 D
- 5/6 C/E *(in any order)*
- 7/8 B/D *(in any order)*
- 9 C
- 10 D
- 11/12 A/B *(in any order)*
- 13/14 A/D *(in any order)*

Vocabulary
2
- a out of practice
- b out of danger
- c out of stock
- d out of the question
- e out of work
- f out of reach
- g out of breath
- h out of sight
- i out of order

Grammar
3
- a a, the
- b –, the
- c the, –, the
- d An, a, the
- e a, the, –
- f –, the, the
- g a, –
- h the, the/–

4
- 1 as
- 2 them
- 3 so
- 4 time
- 5 up
- 6 made
- 7 much
- 8 has
- 9 less
- 10 like

Unit 17
Vocabulary
1
- 1 inclusion
- 2 imaginable
- 3 endless
- 4 competitions
- 5 glamorous
- 6 analysis
- 7 energetic
- 8 unusual
- 9 collection
- 10 Alternatively

2
- a swells
- b cater (for)
- c kick off
- d good causes
- e get hooked
- f bound

3
- a unlikely
- b liking
- c like
- d likeness
- e likeable

Writing
4 **Sample paragraph:**
The haggis, which must be prepared according to the traditional recipe, should be cooled at the time of hurling. The haggis, which will be inspected for illegal firming agents, must not break on landing. A haggis hurler who has the misfortune to see his haggis split will be disqualified. For the junior and middle weight events, where the haggis should weigh approximately 500 grams, the haggis should be no longer than 22 cm with a maximum diameter of 18 cm.

Grammar
5
- 1 it/this
- 2 to
- 3 be
- 4 a
- 5 whose
- 6 all
- 7 no
- 8 as/like
- 9 lot/bit
- 10 where/when
- 11 which
- 12 although/but

Unit 18
Reading
1
- 1 F
- 2 D
- 3 H
- 4 A
- 5 C
- 6 G
- 7 B

Vocabulary
2

F	T	H	R	I	L	L	E	R	A	N	E
I	L	L	U	S	T	R	A	T	I	O	N
C	T	P	A	O	T	C	L	E	O	V	N
T	R	U	C	X	C	H	A	P	T	E	R
I	H	B	T	L	R	A	N	H	I	L	P
O	N	L	I	C	K	R	Y	T	U	I	L
N	B	I	O	G	R	A	P	H	Y	S	O
W	E	S	N	C	S	C	E	N	E	T	T
Y	O	H	R	A	O	T	T	F	T	N	L
K	E	E	H	L	M	E	V	E	N	T	A
X	O	R	A	M	I	R	E	V	I	E	W
W	E	S	T	O	R	Y	O	P	L	A	Y

3 a come up against
  b go under
  c go through
  d go out
  e come down
  f go without
  g go after
  h come out

Grammar

so, such, too, very, enough

4 a such a long book
  b so complicated
  c much too expensive OR too expensive
  d Not enough books were ordered.
  e very sad
  f such an exciting
  g big enough
  h Characters such as these

5 1 very
   2 too
   3 too
   4 very
   5 so
   6 such
   7 enough
   8 such
   9 very
  10 too
  11 so
  12 very
  13 enough
  14 such
  15 too

Unit 19
Reading

1 1 B   2 C   3 D   4 B   5 A   6 D

Vocabulary

2

B	A	N	D	A	G	E	B	H	L
G	N	D	H	W	A	L	L	C	Q
U	K	I	G	I	T	B	K	A	S
F	L	U	U	A	B	O	R	M	T
Y	E	R	O	Y	N	W	T	O	K
M	H	R	C	U	E	N	D	T	N
S	H	A	O	L	X	I	F	S	E
T	E	H	E	A	D	A	C	H	E
Q	R	Y	M	L	D	P	V	N	O
I	N	J	E	C	T	I	O	N	P

Grammar

3 1 high time you stopped
   2 I were you, I would
   3 suggested going/suggested that they (should) go
   4 do you advise me to
   5 to have your teeth checked
   6 (high) time you had/got your
   7 you had better have
   8 had better not sit

Writing

4 *Suggested answer*

Dear Sally,

Thank you for your letter. I'm really looking forward to you coming to stay with me. I went to the local fitness centre and they gave me a leaflet with the information you wanted.

It opens every morning from 6.30 so you will be able to go before work. They say that everyone has to do the introductory session. You can book it when you move in with me. There are discounts but only for the under 18s and the over 60s. You can get a discount if you are a regular user – it's £25 for a week or £65 for a month.

I'm not sure I'll be awake at 6.30 in the morning, but the centre does do dancing classes at the weekend and I think I'd like to do that. Would you like to have a go too? They do salsa, line dancing and jazz dance.

Hope to hear from you soon.

Love,

…………

Unit 20

Vocabulary

1.
   a innocent
   b sentenced
   c witnesses
   d jury
   e defendant
   f evidence
   g fine

2.
   1 illegal
   2 popularity
   3 differences
   4 burglary
   5 evasion
   6 relatively
   7 conventional
   8 increasing
   9 equality
   10 regardless

Idioms

3. 1 e   2 d   3 b   4 f   5 c   6 a

Grammar

4.
   1 what
   2 since
   3 As
   4 ago
   5 the
   6 to
   7 would
   8 her
   9 so
   10 like
   11 on
   12 any/a

Gerund or infinitive

5.
   a He suggested buying a detective novel.
   b I look forward to hearing the results of the case.
   c I enjoy watching American cop programmes. (correct)
   d The burglar alarm needs to be seen to/needs seeing to.
   e Let me give you a description of the mugger.
   f The prisoners were made to sew mail bags. (correct)
   g I can't afford to take a taxi all the time just to avoid the Underground.
   h The tourist was accustomed to driving his car faster in his country.
   i You are not allowed to drop litter on the street.
   j I'd like to report a burglary.
   k She's too small to drive a car. (correct)

Writing

6.
   1 assess   2 document
   3 without   4 written
   5 physical   6 which
   7 consists   8 measurable
   9 although   10 impressively
   11 accepted   12 psychology

Unit 21

Reading

1. He is a rock star, on tour in America.

2. 1 B   2 D   3 A   4 C   5 C   6 B

3.
   a hanging about
   b put off
   c came across
   d fall out with
   e lived up to

Grammar

Conjunctions

4.
   a 5 whereas/while (concessive); so (reason)
   b 8 in case
   c 2 because
   d 1 even though
   e 7 whereas/while (concessive); so (reason)
   f 4 despite/in spite of
   g 3 whereas/while
   h 6 so

Vocabulary

5.
   a balance
   b overdraft
   c interest
   d withdraw
   e capital
   f cashpoint
   g account
   h statement
   i branches
   j debit

Unit 22
Vocabulary

1
1 D	2 B	3 B	4 A
5 C	6 C	7 A	8 B
9 C	10 D	11 A	12 C

2
a performance – not a musical instrument
b conductor – not performing the music but directing it
c festival – more than one event
d key – not something that is composed
e compose – not part of a live performance
f orchestra – much larger group than the others
g stage – something within a physical space
h bass – one instrument as opposed to an orchestra section

Writing

3 1 C 2 E 3 A 4 B 5 F 6 D

Unit 23
Vocabulary

1

Y	L	I	G	H	T	N	I	N	G	N	U
Q	B	D	A	M	P	V	C	A	A	N	P
F	Z	C	V	H	A	I	L	E	L	E	R
L	H	P	O	S	S	W	Q	U	E	F	I
O	X	V	M	R	O	T	S	M	G	L	O
O	Z	Y	J	N	K	O	U	C	L	A	P
D	I	F	S	L	R	E	W	O	H	S	P
S	E	A	Q	I	R	E	D	N	U	H	T
W	G	T	U	F	O	R	E	C	A	S	T
O	I	R	A	I	N	D	R	O	P	R	B
R	S	S	Q	W	P	M	N	E	U	T	Y
H	U	R	R	I	C	A	N	E	E	R	T

Reading

3 a F b F c T d T e T

4
1 C
2 D
3 F
4/5 D/E (in any order)
6 B
7 D
8 A
9/10/11 C/E/F (in any order)
12 G
13/14 A/D (in any order)
15 A

5
a inside g complete
b recalling h occasionally
c enormous i positive
d upper j fit
e sensible/careful k most dangerous
f unlucky l freezing

Grammar

6
a I hope I will see you soon. / I hope to see you soon.
b I wish I could go to visit you.
c Correct
d Correct
e If only you managed to give up smoking, just think of the money you'd save.
f I'd rather stay in a hotel than go camping.
g I hope the weather stays nice for you.
h Correct
i I wish I hadn't seen that film about earthquakes – I can't sleep at night now.
j Correct
k Dave wishes he knew more about earthquakes.
l I would rather you didn't speak to me in that tone of voice.

Unit 24
Grammar

1
1 out
2 like
3 sort/kind/type
4 in
5 this/the
6 a
7 other
8 It
9 too
10 on
11 majority
12 to

76 ANSWER KEY

2   a I don't go to the theatre very often because there isn't one in my town.
    b Could I use your phone, please?
    c Yesterday, I bought her a lovely, blue silk dress. (*Yesterday* can also go at the end)
    d Alan has never been keen on swimming.
    e Quite a few of the members of the audience were students.
    f I like Italian food very much.
    g The crowd watched quietly as they pulled down the old cinema / pulled the old cinema down.
    h The man asked him if he could give him some money.
    i Not only does Alison like bananas/apples, she is also keen on apples/bananas.
    j I have never been so horrified in my life. / Never have I been so horrified in my life.

Vocabulary

Verb collocations

3   a does
    b tastes
    c spend
    d was having
    e sit/keep
    f keep
    g getting
    h broke

Adverb–adjective collocations

4   *highly:* acclaimed; amusing
    deeply: disappointed; ashamed
    perfectly: serious; happy; reasonable
    seriously: ill

5   a deeply disappointed
    b highly amusing
    c perfectly reasonable
    d perfectly serious
    e highly acclaimed
    f deeply ashamed
    g perfectly happy
    h seriously ill

Definitions

6   a a prodigy
    b a portrait
    c priceless
    d scarce
    e garish
    f scepticism
    g sympathetic
    h a colleague

Unit 25

Reading

1   b

2   1 D   2 A   3 B   4 F   5 C   6 G

3

Verb	Noun
adapt	adaptability
harmonise	harmony
locate	location
produce	productivity
promote	promotion
provide	provision, provider
respond	response

Grammar

4   1 e (mixed conditional)
    2 c (second conditional)
    3 a (mixed conditional)
    4 f (third conditional)
    5 d (mixed conditional)
    6 b (mixed conditional)

Vocabulary

5   1 particularly
    2 existence
    3 location
    4 successful
    5 requirements
    6 users
    7 investment
    8 regeneration
    9 unlikely
   10 reconsidered

Unit 26
Grammar

1.
   1. another
   2. when/on/from
   3. since
   4. as
   5. did
   6. be
   7. more/greater
   8. by
   9. must/should
   10. between
   11. not
   12. for

2.
   1. are put at risk
   2. whose aerodynamic fins allow/enable
   3. getting the message across/getting across the message
   4. for whom plans to
   5. get this over with

Vocabulary

3.
   1. B
   2. A
   3. C
   4. B
   5. C (A and B are both used in British English)
   6. A
   7. C
   8. B (radiate)

Writing

4. Corrections are shown in bold:

> **Introduction**
>
> I have been asked to investigate the dangers to **swimmers** who use Whittisham Beach. There have been **several** incidents recently, due to increased use of the sea by jetskis and speedboats.
>
> **The dangers**
>
> Jetskis, whose top speeds are in **excess** of 100kph, come in far **too** close to the shore. As people who swim have their faces under water, they do not **necessarily** see or hear them approaching. Children's **lives** are **especially** endangered, as they are less easy to see. **Until** jetskis are **banned**, people will continue to be put at risk.
>
> I was also informed of an accident **involving** a windsurfer, whose **board** was hit by a motorboat 200 metres out to sea. **Fortunately**, there was no injury to the people involved, but if the motorboat had been going at full speed, the situation would have been much worse.
>
> **Recommendation**
>
> I **believe** Whittisham Council should take urgent action about this. In the short term, notices warning people of the dangers should be placed at both ends of the beach. Of equally high **priority**, councillors must introduce a new policy to limit the use of jetskis and other **pleasure** craft to a safe distance from the beach.

Unit 27
Reading

1. 1 C 2 G 3 B 4 E 5 A 6 D 7 H

Vocabulary

2.
   a. little/no point in
   b. looking for
   c. get round
   d. protected from
   e. deal with
   f. took on

3.
   a. for; after
   b. of
   c. in
   d. at
   e. for
   f. on
   g. between

Grammar

4. Underlined words have been corrected.
   # means an unnecessary word has been removed.

In Mexico you will find <u>many</u> different types of music: traditional, mariachi, boleros, <u>and so on</u>. But the type which young <u>people</u> prefer is # pop-rock. Most of the records they like are about love, their experiences and of course, the problems they see # in society or in the world. The most famous pop singer is Luis Miguel, <u>who</u> has now made many albums. There are also many # women who are famous in our music business. One of them is Shakira and she is one of the best female <u>singers</u> and she also <u>writes her</u> own songs.

Gloria Estefan is internationally famous and she holds <u>a special</u> place in Mexican pop music, <u>even if/although</u> she is from # Cuba, not Mexico. Gloria went to Miami after the Cuban revolution in 1961. In 1975 she sang <u>a lot of/many</u> songs at a wedding. There she met # Emilio Estefan, leader of a band # called The Miami Latin Boys. Soon the band <u>had</u> changed <u>its</u> name to The Miami Sound Machine and by 1983, the group was well known <u>throughout</u> Central and South America. In 1993 Gloria decided to explore her Cuban musical heritage with an album called 'Mi Tierra'. She was chosen # to sing the official theme song of the 1996 Summer Olympics, 'Reach'.

Unit 28

Vocabulary

1 1 b   2 b   3 a   4 a   5 c

2 1 such
   2 times
   3 or
   4 been
   5 the
   6 about
   7 which/that
   8 with
   9 for
   10 to
   11 Although / While / Whereas / Though
   12 not

3 1 impulsive   7 cautious
   2 bored   8 sociable
   3 creativity   9 imagination
   4 distant   10 traditional
   5 dutiful   11 depressed
   6 Safe

Grammar

4 a tights
   b binoculars
   c scissors
   d pyjamas
   e glasses
   f athletics
   g mathematics
   h news
   i politics
   j physics

Writing

5 Complete letter:

> Dear Freda,
> Thank you for your letter. I am/was pleased to hear your news is/was better than the last time you wrote to me. Both my parents send their love.
>
> Last week I bought some new jeans from a new shop in the centre of town. The staff were very helpful. I had to try on eight different pairs because the majority were too tight or not the right colour.
>
> The jeans cost me ninety pounds, which I think isn't too dear for good quality ones. Everybody I know wears designer jeans but my parents think I'm/they're crazy.
>
> Neither my father nor my mother is interested in fashion. All of my mother's clothes are dark blue. I wish she would wear a different colour sometimes!
>
> The real reason I'm writing is to invite you to my birthday party next week. A group of us are going to a new club. Would you like to come? Ring me soon.
>
> Give me regards to your family. I hope they are well.
>
> Love,
>
> Camilla

Unit 29

Reading

1 1 d   2 a   3 e   4 c   5 b

2 1 A   2 D   3 D   4 A   5 C
   6 A   7 C   8 B

Vocabulary

English idioms

3 a keeping my head
   b their feet
   c turned a blind eye
   d the upper hand
   e their fingers burnt
   f eye to eye with
   g turned … its head
   h cold feet

get your **act** together
tighten your **belt**
shocked to the **core**
at a loose **end**
get to **grips** with something
catch someone off **guard**
put something on **ice**
the **icing** on the cake
keep a **low** profile
put your **oar** in
pie in the sky
take somewhere by **storm**
in full **swing**
thin on the ground
go out of the **window**

Unit 30

Vocabulary

1 1 comedians
2 musicians
3 unusual
4 entertainment
5 variety
6 similar
7 products
8 viewers
9 difference
10 endings

2 1 hilarious
2 amusing
3 witty
4 comic

a witty
b Comic; amusing
c hilarious

3 a pay
b court
c pay
d appeared; regular
e not

Grammar

4 1 put up with the tastelessness
2 in clubs rather than
3 put all cigarettes out as/because
4 insisted on knowing the contents
5 had got the sack
6 would rather not stay/wait